DARE TO DREAM

CHANGE-MAKERS, UNSUNG HEROES, INNOVATORS, AND ACHIEVERS THAT MADE US ALL BELIEVE IN DREAMING BIG!

STARDOM BOOKS

STARDOM BOOKS

STARDOM BOOKS

WORLDWIDE

www.StardomBooks.com

STARDOM BOOKS

A Division of Stardom Publishing

and infoYOGIS Technologies.

105-501 Silverside Road

Wilmington, DE 19809

Copyright © 2017 by Stardom Publishing.

All rights reserved, including right to reproduce this book or portions thereof in any form whatsoever.

FIRST EDITION SEPTEMBER 2017

Stardom Books

Dare To Dream: Change-makers, Unsung Heroes, Innovators, And Achievers That Made Us All Believe In Dreaming Big!/

Raam Anand.

p. cm.

1. Business / Self-help / Motivation I. Title

ISBN-13: 978-1976007330

ISBN-10: 197600733X

DEDICATION

This book is dedicated to all those amazing souls who had the guts and perseverance to overcome the insurmountable challenges that life threw at them and survived successfully to tell their stories of what they did more to be more. No wonder it's called "Dare To Dream"!

DISCLAIMER

The views, opinions and information presented in this book are from the co-authors of the publication. The publisher does not endorse or subscribe to the information; reader discretion is solicited.

This book is designed to provide information on how each one of the co-authors did what they did, as their own personal narrative. It is sold with the understanding that neither the co-authors nor the publisher is engaged in rendering legal, accounting or other professional services. If legal or other professional advice is warranted, the services of an appropriate professional should be sought. Also, this book cannot be an exhaustive and complete presentation on the topics within the book. While every effort has been made to make the information presented here as complete and accurate as possible, it may contain errors, omissions or information that was accurate as of its publication but subsequently has become outdated by marketplace or industry changes or conditions, new laws or regulations, or other circumstances.

Neither the co-authors nor the publisher accepts any liability or responsibility to any person or entity with respect to any loss or damage alleged to have been caused, directly or indirectly, by the information, ideas, opinions or other content in this book. If you do not agree to these terms, you should immediately return this book for full refund.

Note from the Publisher

It was a great pleasure to work with all the CO-AUTHORS of this book to bring out their stories, perspectives and insights on how they did what they did.

Each one of them have gone through their own struggles, overcome challenges and successfully steered their businesses and careers into becoming a well-known names in their respective industries.

Through this publication, I wanted to bring out their views so that you, the reader can benefit and get inspired by their achievements. The experts were specifically asked to share how they did they succeed and the stories of their struggles.

So, here it is, for not just your reading pleasure, but also as a reference guide to help you shorten the learning curve and outshine in your own personal endeavors.

As you are going to learn by reading from the contributors of this book, you will understand that all of them have one common thing to say… TAKE ACTION. Go ahead, read the book, take action and bring about a positive difference in your life, business and career – today!

WHEN YOU ARE RIGHT AND OTHERS ARE WRONG…
-- BE FORGIVING AND CONSIDERATE
WHEN YOU ARE WRONG AND OTHERS ARE RIGHT…
-- BE APOLOGETIC AND COURAGEOUS
..BECAUSE IT TAKES A LOT OF COURAGE TO BE SORRY AND APOLOGIZE.

RAAM ANAND, PUBLISHER.

STARDOM BOOKS

CONTENTS

1	FORGE YOUR COURAGEOUS PATH: POWER IN STILLNESS	BY LORA POLOWCZUK	13
2	YES, YOU CAN	By RAMAKANT SHARDA	25
3	THE POWER OF MODELING SUCCESSFUL ATTITUDES AND BEHAVIORS	BY JOHN TERHUNE	37
4	NO BUISINESS FAILS	BY SREEKUMAR VADAKKEPPAT	43
5	THE JOURNEY TO ACHIEVEMENT ...FROM REFUGEE TO RENAISSANCE WOMAN	BY DR. EMILY LETRAN	57
6	IF YOU THINK YOU CAN ..YOU WILL	BY SHEKHAR VIJAYAN	67
7	MY LIFE IS MY MESSAGE THE JOURNEY TO DISCOVERING LIFE'S PURPOSE	BY FAYE KITARIEV	75
8	JOURNALISM JOURNEY TO BECOMING THE CHIEF OF BUREAU	BY SEETHALAKSHMI	87
9	HOW TO COMPETE IN ANY NICHE AND WIN!	BY DOUGLAS KONG	99
10	DON'T SETTLE FOR 7, GO FOR 10!	BY SHANE RAM	107
11	LISTEN! SOMETHING BIG IS CALLING!	BY DIANA DENTINGER	117
12	HOW CONSULTATIVE FINESSE BEATS TYPICAL FIGHT VS. FLIGHT IN STRESSFUL WORK SITUATIONS	BY ROLF FOSTER-JORGENSEN	125

STARDOM BOOKS

ACKNOWLEDGMENTS

You have seen them often. You pick up a book and get to this section, and find that the author, once again, has dedicated the book to someone else and not you. Some unknown, non-existent assistant or some casual reference to famous people.

Not this time.

I would like to thank YOU for taking time to get this book. I would be even more grateful if you read the book and take ACTION to further your life and create a positive difference

1

FORGE YOUR COURAGEOUS PATH: POWER IN STILLNESS
- LORA POLOWCZUK, CHIEF ENERGY OFFICER

An Early Lesson

The thick air was hard to breathe. I could taste the humidity. Sweat bubbled on my skin as I sat thinking on the lush, green grass. It was the peak of summer in Washington, DC, between my junior and senior years of college. With a quick snap, the question "Who's next?" flashed through my mind.

Ten years earlier, my mom quickly had gathered my brother and me and rushed us to the hospital. I saw my father for the last time. In less than six weeks, my father had gone from being my strength to the epitome of frailty. His inoperable lung cancer had spread to his brain. That night, I tried to comfort him the best I could. He died overnight.

This kicked off a chain reaction. My preteen years turned into slow misery. At eleven years old, I slowly lost focus in school and didn't want to be around anyone. I fell into a deep depression. One afternoon, I took a swig of whiskey from the bottle on the kitchen counter before my mom got home from work. I learned that wasn't the best way to cope with pain. It just gave me a horrible headache! With suicidal thoughts rolling in and out of my mind, I comforted myself daily with cookies. This quick deliciousness felt good and numbed the internal pain that tied me up inside. Finally, I cried out for help.

I snapped out of the despair in time for high school. I welcomed the fresh faces and diverse students, the Asians, African-Americans, Latinos, and immigrants.

It was May of my junior year. At 10 p.m., the dreaded phone call came. My best friend had been-boned in a car accident. I rushed to the hospital. Another life lost too soon. I was devastated. Depression set in again. I broke free shortly before college started.

I pursued a neuroscience degree. I was fascinated with the scientific basis of behavior: why we do certain things, why we move certain ways, and why I was able to beat depression while others had not.

As my mind stilled on that hot summer day, it was as if a light bulb turned on. I realized something very important. My father died at age forty-nine. My best friend died at eighteen. It was a harsh reality check. My thought pattern immediately changed. Life is short. You never know when your time will be up. Life took on new meaning. Did I use to ask, Why? Now I ask, Why not? From that day forward, depression never crept back into my life again. Life is here to be lived.

Stillness Moment #1: Life is short. Ask Why not? instead of Why?

Pivot

This theme continued: Do what you want! I bustled through college and gathered all the opportunities I could. I became a teaching assistant. I conducted research in both psychology and neuroscience and presented at prestigious national and international conferences. I experienced more than most students. Yet I was tired and needed a break. This led me to my first life pivot. The idea of continuing with a six-year Ph.D. program no longer excited me.

Stillness Moment #2: Take stock of your situation, recognize what you don't want, and move out of the situation.

Exploration Begins

After college graduation, I explored Europe with a friend. With only a backpack, a few clothing items, and a travel book, we set out on a massive adventure for one month. (This was before the Euro existed and international cell phones worked!)

From getting kicked out of a nun's convent in Venice, Italy, to a train ride through the vastness of the Swiss Alps, to an impromptu visit to a music festival in Nice, to exploring the vast living arrangements of nobility in Versailles, France, the experiences were more than I could imagine. My taste buds popped from new foods. My mind expanded from the museums. New perspectives emerged as I learned what was important in each culture and accepted them as they were. The whole trip taught us to be flexible. Sometimes the railway goes on strike and you can't get from Point A to Point B. Life doesn't always go as expected. It's learning how not to be reactive that's important. Take stock of the situation and adjust your course. We have a choice. We can't get all flabbergasted when things don't go as expected. Sit down and methodically think, What are my options from here? Let it be an informed response, not a reaction.

I created memories and experiences with hardly any money at all. Since then, I've made a point to travel internationally almost every year. I've traveled to over seventeen countries and six continents.

Stillness Moment #3: Recognize you have a choice.

Believe in Your Work

From behavioral interventions for heroin addiction to conducting clinical trials for psychiatric drugs, I enjoyed designing research studies, analyzing data, and exploring how to make systems efficient. I fell in love with bringing prevention efforts and treatments to those in need. I obtained a Masters in Public Health degree from the elite Johns Hopkins University.

I prided myself on connecting colleagues with project updates and timelines that affected them. This built trust that colleagues would never be undercut or deal with something unexpected. I communicated deficiencies or potential problem areas and offered solutions where possible. I always wanted to stay on top of my game.

I combined my love of public health and travel and delved into global infectious diseases by conducting malaria vaccine trials for a non-profit. I marveled at how I could combine both passions. I was impressed by how much coordination and communication public-private partnerships entailed. For one clinical trial, we had multiple buy-ins from clinical sites and tribal leaders in Africa, our funding partners, a pharmaceutical company, and the U.S. military. This came in handy when I later collaborated on global health policy matters at the highest levels of the U.S. government for preventing and intercepting global pandemics.

As my career soared, I offered to lead new initiatives and was always assigned highly visible projects, each of which made a big impact. I wanted to make a difference.

Stillness Moment #4: Belief in what you spend your time on.

Take Opportunities

When you're young, you think you're invincible. Until one day, your company lays you off. Luckily, the first time it happened, I had a nine-month heads-up. While my colleagues freaked out, I gladly looked at this as an opportunity to evaluate my options. I didn't feel I had to rush to find a new job as I was getting a hefty payout for staying until the end. Out of 150 people, most of whom either left early with no extra money or relocated to the new city, I was the only person who took two months off. My first sabbatical in my mid-twenties! How cool was that! I used the time to travel abroad for the first time alone to Australia and New Zealand and complete my Masters in Public Health Degree. I'm one of the few Americans to take vacation time every year. It's not about what society wants you to do (go make money!); it's about what you want to do. For me, this was travel, exploration, and outdoor adventures.

Stillness Moment #5: Trust in the opportunity. You never know where it will take you.

Keep Your Passion for Work in Check

I kept looking for more, to achieve more, until it did me in. As I rose through the ranks, my passion for my work was a double-edged sword. In interviews, I would express that dedication was my best and worst trait. I wanted to be seen as capable of doing it all. I moved from operations to the strategist and visionary for companies. I executed projects and could pinpoint the risk factors and solve them before they became big problems. Yet personally, I became unfocused. It was hard to keep up with everything.

I could already recognize burnout (mental and physical exhaustion), and I attempted to prevent it. Yet I began a series of burnout positions, in which I worked constantly to prove myself. The harder I tried, the worse the job became. After one position ended, I embarked on a three-month spiritual journey through Asia. It took that long for my body to recuperate and lose the twenty pounds I had gained in six months. I desperately wanted to feed my soul again.

Stillness moment #6: Work to live. Don't live to work.

As I went through my career in the medical, healthcare, and

public health arenas, I worked a lot of hours. I supplemented the energy with a lot of caffeine and sugar. Over the course of my career, I wrecked my body three times. Each of these burnouts caused major inflammation in my body. To this day, even though I'm still relatively young, I have to deal with this on a daily basis. I realized I need to treat my body like a temple. The food we put in our body and the hours we work can cause stress and impact how we function. I didn't have the best mindset.

While I had had amazing positions working on global pandemics and emerging diseases, they somehow weren't satisfying. I was restless and unfulfilled in life despite an amazing resume full of accolades, accomplishments, and amazing references. I always threw myself into my job at the sacrifice of everything else. I longed for more connection, time with friends, relaxation, and fun. I squeezed in quick exploration trips whenever I could.

Stillness moment #7: Recognize that why you are doing something should be bigger than what you're sacrificing.

How Nature Nurtured Me
After getting out of a long relationship, I joined an outdoor club to meet new people and try new activities. I started with short hikes, which led to longer hikes, which led to steeper hikes. I loved the social aspect and challenged myself to attempt something harder. I wondered where I would go. I enjoyed being outside. It was peaceful being away from a computer and the cell phones hardly worked. It was the downtime I needed from all the work.

Stillness moment #8: Disconnect to Connect.

Break Out of Your Shell
I attempted rock climbing and fell in love. It was one more thing to do outside. A couple years later, I tried ice climbing. Six months later, I embarked on a mountaineering trip to Mt. Rainier.

Each courageous step built upon the last. As an unathletic kid, I had never had a clue that one day I would climb frozen waterfalls for the fun of it and I would become an ice climber. Who knew?

Climbing built my courage to believe in myself and to trust in others. The mental part was key. This is where it also built my confidence. It's all up to you whether or not you reach for that next move. No one is pushing you. Friends might be encouraging you, but it's up to you yourself to do pull the move. We have to take those same courageous moments, as I do in climbing, and apply them to the rest of our lives. Because the one thing I can tell you is that when I'm doing a lot of courageous outdoor activities, I am very courageous in the rest of my life. It's a parallel, and this is what I love about the outdoors.

The aspect I love about climbing is that it's a puzzle. The idea is to get to the top of the climb. It's up to you to figure out the puzzle to get there, and it's the same metaphor for life. We may have our starting point here, and our goal is over there, but it's that same puzzle. You may not see each step, each hole, each hand or foot placement the entire way up from the bottom, but as you start to move, each step appears, showing you where to go, where the next piece is. It's similar to life. It's about taking that leap of faith, not knowing the outcome until the answer suddenly appears.

There are also times with climbing when you hit a barrier. You get stuck, and you have to sit and troubleshoot where you are. It's the same in life. You may come to a fork in the road. You must get still and carefully assess your options.

Climbing became my moving meditation. It gave me the focus to tune everything else out and to carefully assess where I need to go for the next move, even if I didn't know what was next.

Stillness moment #9: Where do you expand your comfort zone and take a leap of faith into something new?

Ready to Change

To keep going all day long and not take breaks, I was overcaffeinating and eating sugary pastries. I didn't take ownership of what I was eating and wasn't moving my body enough (i.e., exercising). I used food for energy instead of generating my own. The over-caffeinated blew out my adrenal glands. What I realize now is that when I was working fifty, sixty, and, at times, even eighty hours a week, I wasn't being true to myself or to what I love to do, like being outdoors. While I made a point to climb outdoors weekly for almost ten years, it wasn't enough self-care time. Neither were quick three-day trips to New England to ice climb and four-day trips to the Rocky Mountains to ski. The hustle and bustle finally caught up with me.

I continued to work long hours. I started learning about high-performance mindset and habits but hadn't implemented it yet. I went from an epic two-week alpine climbing trip in Ecuador climbing seventeen-thousand-foot peaks to complete and utter exhaustion a year later. I gained twenty pounds in one year yet again and could only function enough to travel to a beach in Mexico and sleep all day for a week. A couple months later, my body was not equipped for a four-day ski trip, and I severely injured my knee and required surgery. My body had given up.

This was my third burnout. It was time to break the cycle. Enough was enough.

Stillness moment #10: Identify the pattern and readjust your path

The Birth of Coaching and the Movement Paradox™

I realized I inspired others when I lived my outdoor passions and traveled the world. Anyone can do this if they focus their intentions on it. It became my mission to show other high achievers that working long hours is not a badge of honor. The consequences are real. I began implementing high-performance techniques, and the results were outstanding. I got more done in one day than during the whole of the prior month. I became a coach to share this.

Nature is my challenge and my serenity. I move out of my comfort zone and test my capabilities in new terrain. Yet, at the same time, I enjoy the beauty and awe of the stunning environment I am surrounded by. It's moving and getting still concurrently. This is true in life, as well. This is where the Movement Paradox™ was birthed: that we simultaneously make bold, challenging moves, yet we need to stop, look up, and appreciate is around us. This allows us to assess: Are we on the right path? Are we going around the mountain, or are we headed up the mountain? What do clues tell us if this is the right direction? On a hike, it's very easy to look at your feet for a couple hours without looking up and seeing the magnificent scenery that's before your eyes. It's the same metaphor for life. Don't keep moving so fast that you forget to celebrate all the milestones along the way. What is your vision? Are you only looking at right now, the next step, or are you looking at the bigger picture, the bigger vision of your life?

The Movement Paradox™, when implemented, creates a life full of freedom, meaningful experiences, and serving the world in an impactful way. Freedom is about having clarity in who you are and who you want to become. It's about taking ownership for your choices. Life is about taking responsibility for two of our most precious resources: our time and energy. Instead of burnout, we can choose a life that brings meaning, impact, and fulfillment.

Meaningful experiences show up in how you choose to interact with yourself, others, and the world around you. When we fully engage ourselves and others, not a half-hearted effort, we create deep, rich connections and daily meaningful interactions. This, in turn, impacts those around us; our friends, our family, our colleagues, our communities, our country, and even our world. How do you want to be remembered?

Stillness Moment #11: Get Still and Reflect Daily

Do your daily life choices honor who you want to become?
Are you deliberately focused on a few projects that propel your

life forward? Do you execute these projects efficiently to avoid a sense of overwhelming and frustration?

Do you incorporate daily self-care to protect your own energy reservoir so you can serve greatly without exhausting yourself?

Do your attitude and conversations reflect the best of who you are on a daily basis?

Do you take courageous steps to grow?

Movement without stillness leads to overwhelming, burnout, and unfulfillment. Instead of constantly moving without thought, get still. If we get still, each experience fosters the opportunity to move intentionally and forge our own courageous path.

Sign-Up for the pdf download: 5 Tips to Gain an Extra Hour in Your Day at bit.ly/5tipsTime

Follow Lora Polowczuk, Chief Energy Officer at Courageous Path at:
www.courageouspath.net
https://twitter.com/courageous_path
https://www.instagram.com/courageous.path/
https://www.facebook.com/courageouspath/

© Courageous Path

Lora Polowczuk

Lora Polowczuk, Chief Energy Officer at Courageous Path, is a high-performance coach and trainer. She catapults overwhelmed high achievers from stressed out and unfulfilled workers into vibrant, efficient, and engaged superstars in work, life, and play. She wants you to have time and energy for your passions and loved ones. Lora facilitates coaching programs, training programs, and outdoor retreats.

After multiple burnouts, Lora stopped the craziness and developed key, proven processes to maintain high-performance, joy, and harmony. Her motto is "Stop Burnout. Start Living."

Lora's Movement Paradox™ paradigm shows you how to experience connection and harmony. This paradigm depicts how courage bridges bold moves and self-reflection to create a fulfilled, meaningful, and impactful life without getting burned out in the process. She ignites her client's potential through values-based decision making. As clients align their true essence with their actions, they learn how to set boundaries, increase their self-confidence, communicate effectively, live in the flow instead of a reactive state, speak their voice, and manage time efficiently to live an empowered life and career. By the end, clients gain a sense of freedom and renewed energy to fully live their dreams and increase their performance.

Lora is an Associate Certified Coach through the International

Coach Federation and Certified High Performance Coach. Lora received a Masters of Public Health from Johns Hopkins University and a Bachelor's of Science in neuroscience from the University of Scranton. Lora believes coaching facilitates optimum changes in the brain, which in turn creates forward-thinking, positive performance change, and healthy behaviors.

Lora's dynamic and forward-thinking nature draws from a wealth of diverse perspectives spanning academic research, a private sector, non-profits, public-private partnerships, government policy, and entrepreneurship. After enduring the loss of loved ones early in life, she adopted the attitude that life is short, and she expresses gratitude for each moment, no matter the outcome. Her love of travel and outdoor adventure shaped her beyond her wildest dreams, from climbing the seventeen-foot mountain in South America, to extensive independent travel in Asia. Her style is not why, but why not? Lora brings enthusiasm, energy, and a zest for life to show clients that infinite possibilities exist and anything is possible.

When Lora's not serving her clients, you can find her hiking in the Rocky Mountains near her home in Colorado, scaling a rock cliff, or skiing down a mountain. Nature and travel are where her heart thrives.

2

YES, YOU CAN
HAVE FAITH AND TURN YOUR BIGGEST DREAMS INTO REALITY
- BY RAMAKANT SHARDA, APPRENEUR

I wasn't born with a golden spoon in my mouth, or even a silver one actually, and life was never easy for me. No doubt, it has given me so many good things, but most of the time, it took them back.

So why I am telling you this? Just to prove that in spite of all odds, you can still achieve your dreams. No matter what your current situation is, where you are, how old you are, how difficult your life seems to you at this moment, you can still have dreams and manifest them into reality.

Let me take you back a few years in time. I was 12years old. One day, I realized that my singing voice was exceptional. I caught myself singing, and I was really good. A few days later, I was in a cultural event at a place just behind my home. It was 3:00 am, and I was sitting there in the hope that I might get a chance to sing. Luckily, I got it when someone started singing a very typical bhajan (devotional song) but couldn't sing it properly. When I asked to be allowed to sing this bhajan, everyone started laughing at me.

Imagine a 12-year-old kid who looks eight, claiming to sing a bhajan that regular singers couldn't sing. But when I started singing, everyone was stunned, and one person even rushed to my home to wake up my parents. It was like a magical moment in my life. Suddenly I had become a celebrity.

Within a year I become a renowned singer. I was being specially invited to big programs for my talent. A Good Samaritan once even convinced me that my voice was so good that I could make my own bhajan album. He said that he had good connections and he'd help me release my album.

I felt like I could jump and touch the stars—but life wanted something else from me, and within a few days of his offer, my voice started getting hoarse without any reason. I tried to improve it. I visited some doctors but in vain. Within the next two months, I lost my singing voice. I went into a depression, and there was nobody to support me. It took me many years to overcome the depression and the associated trauma. In hindsight, I think I have learned a lot from that experience, which boils down to:

"Don't struggle to change bad things which are not in your control, just accept it and let go."

In 1994, an industrialist offered me to become a partner in his business. I don't know why, but he was very impressed with me. I was like on cloud nine. Imagine you are just 18 years old and you have become a partner with big industrialist. We started working together, but very soon afterward, the factory workers went on strike. To my dismay, the debacle extended for a long time, with neither party agreeing to come to terms, eventually leading to my partner going bankrupt. He had no option but to run away from the business, and I was left with my first bitter taste of business failure and lots of debt.

In order to repay my debts, I started a new business. Initially, it went really well, but before I had some good breakthroughs, the government changed a policy, and within a day my business came crashing down to zero!

Inevitably, I had to join my family business, only to get extremely bored within a year. The fire and the urge to do something on my own was burning inside me, and I decided to start a new journey. A new adventure which I could call my own.

My life lesson so far was: **"When things don't go according to you, lower your expectations. Keep your dreams BIG but lower the expectation of outcome."**

I tried a few businesses, but none of them worked out well for me. Then I come to know about a Malaysian company, which deals in health care products that are based on infrared therapy. I started working for on it. This business started taking off slowly, and soon I was racing toward the top. I made my own presentation slides and started touring the entire state of Rajasthan, presenting my slides. I went a little bit further and even compiled a book on the benefits of infrared therapy.

A top leader of the company noticed my efforts, and he was very impressed with me and supported me in a big way. Soon I was driving a Mercedes-Benz and had a big office in a posh area of the city. Everything was going well, and I was feeling like I was on the top of the world again.

This, too, was about to come crashing down. Once again, life wasn't fair towards me. One day I had severe stomach ache during work, and it turned out to be diagnosed as appendicitis. I had to go for surgery, and I couldn't go to the office for ten days. When I returned to the office, a big shock was waiting for me. In such a short span of time, everything had been changed. A member of my own team, in whom I had put a lot of faith, and trusted, had turned against me. He had also poisoned the minds of other team members, they all started annoying me with unfair demands.

I tried to manage but couldn't. Therefore, I decided that since I had been able to make this team, I could make another one again. I started working on that but my mentor, who was supporting me, left the company and later committed suicide. It was a major setback for me as we were good friends too. After another six months of struggle, I decided to leave that business.

It was time to do shift my focus. During that exact time, online business models had started booming. Therefore, I planned to go with the flow.

Lesson learned: **"Sometimes things may not go as you planned. Accept it, move on, and go with the flow."**

In 2002, I started an e-commerce site to sell Indian handicraft products in the US and other countries. I made the website and started sourcing products. Meanwhile, one of my acquaintances came to know about my website and offered to become a partner in the business. We became partners and decided that my team's job would be to do marketing and get orders and his part of the work would be to source products and ship them.

Soon our business took off, and we started getting orders. The first 2-3 months, everything went smoothly. Then the troubles started. My partner started acting erratically and wouldn't handle orders properly or ship the items on time. I had to jump back in and take care of his part of the workload too.

Finally, I told him that we couldn't work like this. I offered to him that either he paid me my initial investment and bought the site or I'd pay him his investment and take over the business. He agreed to withdraw, I returned his investment and was now the whole and sole owner of this business. Pretty comfy, right?

This new change came with new problems. Most of the suppliers had come from the efforts of my ex-partner, and they started troubling me. Sometimes, they intentionally delayed deliveries and I had to struggle to find other suppliers at short notice.

Then I faced the most challenging problem. My site got hacked, and hackers kept on changing everything on my site, including images, descriptions, and even prices. I don't know if they were doing this just for fun, as they didn't demand any money from me. I hired three different companies, but none of them could beat the hackers. Eventually, I had to shut down my site and once again, I was jobless with one more failure on my hands.

Next, I started selling products on Baazee.com. It was late 2003—I started with handicraft products, but soon I changed it to eBooks and info products. Within three months I was among top sellers of Baazee.com. I was selling a huge number of eBooks daily, my costs were zero, and I needed to send only a download link to my buyers. There was no investment, no stock, no packing, and no shipping. Yippee!

All I had to do was to check my emails in the morning to know how many orders I had, send them an email with the download link, and I was done. Whatever money I got from Baazee.com was pure profit.

Lesson learned: **"Sometimes success doesn't come from where you expect it, it comes from where you least expect it."**

This was the easiest business I have done to date, but as usual, it didn't last long. Baazee.com was acquired by eBay, and the very first thing they did was to shut down the info product category, and my business vanished overnight. Ouch!

One good thing that happened in my life was that whenever I faced failure, the next thing I got was usually bigger and better than the previous one. By this time, I knew that online business was the future and info products were the best things to sell online.

I started learning about online business. During those times, there was only dial-up Internet available in India, and it wasn't cheap. The tariff was cheaper from midnight to early morning, so I started working from 11:00 in the night till 5:00 in the morning.

Sometimes we wish that we had the power to go back in our life and change some past decisions. Don't you feel the same? Actually, I do feel it for my education. I am from a business family and from my childhood, I always thought of doing business. At the age of 14, I started earning money by making electromagnets, kaleidoscopes and other science projects, and selling them in school, so I always thought that it was better for me to take commerce as a major for graduation. Now I think that if I had taken up engineering, things would have been different in my life. Unfortunately, we don't have such power and nothing can be done now.

Anyways, by the end of 2004, I started my own eZine and entered into the online info products business. Again, it wasn't so easy for me, as at that time, Indian merchants had a bad reputation and most companies didn't accept Indians as their clients. Most of the marketers refused to do joint ventures with me because I was an Indian merchant.

I still remember that when I wanted to open an account with a payment processor, they wouldn't allow Indians. I had to give them an assurance in writing, that "let me open an account and work for 2-3 months, and after that if they thought that I am legitimate, they'd continue - otherwise they might close my account and forfeit all my earnings.

I started working under such harsh conditions and slowly started building my reputation amongst other marketers. In March 2005, I got an idea for a piece of software and started working on it. It was ready by June. I launched this project, and it got unexpected success.

As usual, my bad luck struck again, and a person came from nowhere and accused me of stealing his idea. I checked his site and investigated deeply to find clues to prove that his software was created later, and he was lying that I had stolen his idea and I proved it successfully. But he went further and got my PayPal account closed with this lie. Since I was from India and he was from the US, he had the advantage, and my account was shut down. He also tried to shut down my site, but fortunately, my server company took my side and didn't do it.

Anyways, I needed to move to another payment processor, and I found one. Frankly, these are a few small number of failures I faced. If I try to remember and write all the failures and setbacks, probably I'd need to write a whole book.

I started working on other projects, and 2006 was my best year for online business. Almost every month I launched a new project, and most of my projects become ultra-successful. I achieved many unexpected targets, I did joint ventures with most of the industry leaders, and by the end of 2006, I was among the top Internet marketers in the world.

Lesson learned: **"When you believe, good things happen automatically."**

Until 2006, I was too busy in a cycle of repeated failures, but then my life became stable, so I decided to live according to my philosophy of a "Balanced Life Formula." I strongly believe that four pillars support a good, happy life, and in order to live a fulfilled life you need to balance all four pillars and give equal importance to all. These pillars are:

- You (your hobbies and things that give you true happiness)
- Family / Friends
- Health
- Money (your business/job)

I observed that the majority of people are usually giving most of their attention to only one pillar. Yes, you guessed it right—it's money. They sacrifice their relationship and even their health to earn money. They don't even remember what their hobbies are, or what gives them true happiness.

They spend their entire life believing that once they have plenty of money, they will be happy. No doubt, money is important to live a good life, but it's not everything. Actually, money has a quality—the more you have it, the more you want it, and it's a never-ending cycle, which doesn't allow you to get out of the race. I am not trying to change the world but what I strongly believe is that:

"Balancing a checkbook is not enough; balancing life while balancing a checkbook is more important."

So, I started regular workouts and meditation. I spared some time for my hobbies and also started spending more time with friends. I also set up a period of uninterrupted quality time with my family every day.

The word "family" means a lot to me; it's my small and beautiful world within this world. I am lucky to have my beautiful wife Seema, who is the strength for me and has stood by me in every up and down of my life. Many times, I have had to take hard decisions, but she has always supported me. Kanishka and Lakshya are my two cute kids. Kanishka is 15 and Lakshya is 10. As a parent, I am trying to teach my children about living a balanced life, to always dream big, but to not get attached to it, and to live each and every moment joyfully and peacefully. I want to make them understand that:

"Life is like a journey and your dreams and goals are your destinations. Don't think that you'll start enjoying your life only after reaching your destination. So many beautiful things will come on the path toward your dreams. Don't miss them, be in that moment, and enjoy them too."

Photography was one of my hobbies from childhood, but I couldn't pursue it due to all those problems. Wait—it's not just a hobby. Actually, it's my life. It's like meditation for me, which calms me down and gives me extreme joy. Anyways, now it was time to work on it, and today I can proudly say that I've made quite a good name in photography. I've released three coffee table books, and my work has been published in many photography magazines, newspapers, and lots of international sites.

I've read somewhere that "Happiness comes when you accept whatever is going in your life and you live in the current moment, not a moment in the past, and not a moment in the future." True, but I also believe that:

"True happiness comes when you live a balanced life."

OK, back to the story. In 2009, the same thing happened one more time. My father got hospitalized due to some serious problems, and I had to take care of him and his business for six months. During that period, I lost control over my own business, my list of over 60,000 subscribers suddenly become non-responsive, the projects I was working on got delayed or never took off, and like the previous times, everything slipped from my hands, and I couldn't do anything.

In 2011, I started again from zero and this time I entered the mobile app publishing business because I realized mobile was the next wave. One of my passions is to help people live a peaceful and joyful life. I am trying to do it with my apps, and the best part about the app business is that I can have global reach and help anyone who is ready to change.

I made many games and then I launched a series of five apps called "30 Days to Become a Better xxxxxx". These apps provide a simple task to do every day for 30 days and if someone does these regularly, they can become a better father, mother, husband, wife, or photographer. I think these five apps are the best in my entire apps portfolio.

People who are using these apps have experienced a great improvement in their life, especially in relationships. When someone sends me a thank you message about how their life and relationship have improved after using one of my apps, it gives me a feeling of fulfillment. If you can change someone's life for the better, it's the best job in the world.

Lesson learned: **"No matter in what circumstances you are in, if you have faith, you can achieve anything."**

I am not a multi-millionaire, and I haven't created a billion-dollar company yet, but I am living a balanced and peaceful life, I am healthy, I always feel free, happy, and joyful. Most people are running blindly without knowing where they want to go, but I know what my dreams are, I am working slowly to achieve them, and one by one my dreams are becoming my reality.

My number one dream was to become a published author, though I didn't know how it was going to be possible. But my strong belief that one-day it would happen for sure has made this my reality, and with this book, today I can proudly say that I've accomplished it.

Lesson learned: **"Don't give up on your dreams, no matter what."**

I think we all have a super-human power and that is the power of belief. If you truly believe something, it happens for sure. I have this power, and you—yes, you too—have it. And everyone else on this planet also has it. Use this power and make your life wonderful.

I've learned so many lessons in this life, and I've tried to incorporate most of them in my story. I hope you are going to love it.

Since my biggest dream, which seemed extremely tough earlier, has come true now, I am daring to pursue my wildest dream, which is impossible to achieve logically—at least according to three doctors I've discussed it with. But I have faith that one day I'll achieve it too. So wish me luck, and keep doing good work and achieve your goals and dreams. All the best.

"Dream big, have faith and life will find a way."

Ramakant Sharda

Ramakant Sharda is an appreneur based in the beautiful "Pink City" of India, known as Jaipur. He creates games and lifestyle apps for iPhone and iPad. He is trying to help people live a happy life with his "30 Days" app series.

Photography is one of his passions and he is quite good at it—his work has been published in various magazines, newspapers, and blogs. He writes about photography and also teaches photography in his workshops.

For more information, please visit
www.kiplapps.com
www.clickmanic.com

3

THE POWER OF MODELING SUCCESSFUL ATTITUDES AND BEHAVIORS
- BY JOHN TERHUNE, PEOPLE SKILLS & ATTITUDE EXPERT

When I was asked to author a chapter of this book and tell you about me, I felt a bit uncomfortable. This feeling came from the fact that I really don't like talking about me. I would much rather focus on "the other person" and help the other person understand how special they are in our world. Nonetheless, the request caused me to pause and reflect on my life.

As I write this chapter, I am a very young and very happy sixty-four-year young man. I have been happily married (to the same woman) for thirty-three years. I have three fantastic children and four absolutely remarkable grandchildren who know me as Papa John. I am in great physical shape, due to extreme discipline in the areas of eating and exercise and I own multiple businesses that create a phenomenal lifestyle for my family and myself. I have been blessed to have visited over thirty different countries, I have seen the world as few will ever do and I have been privileged to have created experiences for my wife and my kids and now grandkids that will be memories that will last their lifetime. I can't tell you how many times when I am reading a book, or watching a movie that the scenes of the movie or book are places I have been; often times with my family alongside me. Today I have dreams every bit as big as they were when I was a much younger man chronologically and I awake each day mission and dream driven. I am always excited knowing that I am a center of influence with my family, my colleagues and my family. I know every day that my life is being watched and that the actions of my life are influencing the people I cross paths with in life. How do I know that? Because that is how my life became so great. I watched my parents as I was a child instilled in me the attributes that define my life today.

I grew up as the eldest child (I have three siblings) of a military officer. The life of a military officer is one that requires regular moves from one post to the next. Until I was in college I had never gone to one school two years in a row because we were constantly moving. Some people may view that as a negative. Not for me. It turned out to be a great blessing because it made me able to adjust and make new friends very easily. That trait has continued with me and has served me very well through the years.

My parents were married for almost 60 years before their passing over the last several years. I witnessed throughout my childhood a loving, respectful relationship between two best friends. The positive nature of their relationship was imprinted in my soul as a child. My wife and I have always sought to do the same for our children. I am pleased to say that as proud as I am of each of my children for so many things, I am most proud of them because they are fantastic parents to their children. Isn't it amazing how your attitudes and behaviors can become your legacy through the people who are watching you?

There were other amazing influences from my relationship with my parents that defined my life. One was that both my Mother and father had an incredible work ethic. I spent my childhood seeing my father leave the house at 6 am or earlier and not be home until well into the evening. Even when he retired from the military, he took on a civilian job with the same dedication for an additional twenty years. Day after day, week after week, month after month, year after year.

Additionally, both of my parents encouraged dreaming beyond your current circumstances. From my childhood those dreams were not discouraged as impossible from my parent's language, they were encouraged as being completely possible. Since I have been a kid, I have been in the passionate pursuit of my dreams and it has added purpose and vision to my life at every stage. With my parents it was never whether you could fly, it was about how high could you fly. Their words and belief in me acted as a constant wind beneath my wings in my pursuits.

My first adult dream to move my life forward was to become a great trial lawyer. After graduating with honors from College, I was accepted to a very prestigious Law School; Florida State University. I was privileged to be selected to their "Moot Court Team" of advocates would compete against other Law Schools. In my third and final year of Law School, I was named by the American Trial Lawyers Association as the Best Student Trial Advocate in a Nationwide competition.

Upon graduation, I became a prosecuting attorney for the State of Florida. In that capacity, I handled most of the murder and significant felony crimes in my jurisdiction. In a ten-year career, I handled over 5000 criminal cases and won 97% of the more than 200 trials that I tried in front of a jury, earning me a top rating as a lawyer.

After a decade of being a prosecuting attorney, I was growing restless with my career path. Although I enjoyed my job, my dreams were far bigger than the job could pay. So I took a risk and transitioned my career into business consulting, business coaching and keynote speaking. In so doing for the first time I began to feel the freedom that comes when you have decided to define your own destiny by owning your future. I embraced entrepreneurship with everything I had. No longer was someone else defining my worth. My worth was now being defined by how hard I was willing to work and how creative I could become in helping other people solve relevant issues in their life.

As I worked with more and more people around the world in my capacities as a keynote speaker, consultant, and coach, I began to realize that I had a gift. That gift was to help people understand and reach their full potential. I find it so sad that so few people truly understand let alone reach their full potential. My mission in life is to get them to clearly understand who they are in this universe and that they can change the world if they believe it. Then my mission transitions to helping those people create the personal tool set of skills and attitudes that will enable their potential to be achieved. It has been an absolute rule that I have seen over and over again that helps me create focused content and trainings for people who want to live an extraordinary life. In my life's experiences, a person has to develop themselves in four key areas to ever reach their full potential. Those areas are Attitude, Leadership, People Skills and Team Work. If a person sharpens their "personal sword" in these areas and then combines those skills with a vision, massive focus, a defined process and then accountability, there is no limit on the potential of a human being.

As I close out this chapter, I have two very important thoughts for you to ponder. First, I am very sensitive to the fact that not everyone was blessed with the loving childhood that I was blessed to enjoy. I run into so many people who never received the encouragement or examples of positive attitudes and behaviors that set the foundation for the successes in my life. In fact, many people had just the opposite. If that is your case, let me encourage you to know that you are in fact special. You are in fact extraordinary. You are a gift to the world. You have it in you to change the world. It is to you as a birth right as a human being. I encourage you, don't allow yourself to be the victim. Decide to be the victor. End this chapter knowing that I believe in you and your potential and know that you can be a positive force and example to others.

Lastly, I talk often about the intersection of preparation and opportunity. When intelligent, focused preparation in building an extraordinary you are matched with the right moment of opportunity, life changing things can happen for you and the people in your life who mean the most to you. We are living in a time where opportunity is not "knocking at your door," it is literally knocking down the walls of your house. My colleague Les Brown has an awesome statement to remember. "It is better to be prepared and lacks opportunity than it is to have the opportunity present itself and you are not prepared."

You my friend and the way that you think is your single greatest asset. Invest time and money to build a better you. It is a lifelong project. Achievement rarely happens without the predicate of becoming. Focus on becoming and watch how "lucky" finds you with life changing opportunity. Can't wait to hear how you changed the world.

John Terhune

John Terhune's riveting and passionate programs have made him one of the world's most in-demand speakers. He has shared the stage with Presidents Ronald Reagan and Gerald Ford; General Norman Schwarzkopf and Colonel Oliver North; football legends Coach Tom Landry and Joe Theisman; and inspirational and motivational figures such as Dr. Norman Vincent Peal, John Maxwell, and Zig Ziglar.

John has authored multiple books on success principles in business and life to include his favorite subjects of entrepreneurship, attitude development, and people skills. One of the most important hats he wears is that of an Attitude Coach. In fact, in the last 20 years, he has been an Attitude Coach for thousands of people around the world including entrepreneurs and corporate executives in 18 different countries.

Where It All Began John was raised as the eldest child of a military officer. Moving almost every year until entering college gave John the ability to make friends quickly and to relate to a wide spectrum of people very naturally. To this day he credits the experience of having to make john-speak new friends every year as an important contributing factor to his highly developed people skills.

His dream early in life was to become a trial attorney. After graduating with honors from the University of South Florida in Tampa, John was accepted into the prestigious Florida State Law School in Tallahassee Florida. While at FSU Law School John was a member of the elite Moot Court Team and in his third year won the title of Top Trial Advocate in a National competition sponsored by the American Trial Lawyers Association. Upon graduation from FSU Law School, John went on to a career as an Assistant State Attorney for the State of Florida. During his decade long career as a prosecutor, he earned top ratings as an attorney heading up the felony division of his circuit in North Florida handling over 5,000 criminal cases and winning 97% of the over 200 cases that he tried relaxed-john-round-shadows before juries.

While serving as the Chief Felony Prosecutor, John was also an adjunct instructor teaching Criminal Law, Business Law and Evidence at multiple colleges. John is a passionate husband of more than thirty years, father to three wonderful children and proud grandfather to two beautiful grandchildren.

4

NO BUSINESS FAILS
- SREEKUMAR VADAKKEPPAT

As humans, it would be out of line to think that we could thrive for very long without learning a thing or two from each other. From the time we were born, we have always learned one thing or the other from our parents, other members of the family, relatives, and friends. This is simply a fact of life, there is no running around this.

Learning should, therefore never be seen as a sign of weakness, rather it shows great strength. If an individual remains committed to developing himself as a human being, despite the basic challenges of life, such a fellow has truly exhibited great strength. Even in the face of unfavorable experience, he remains committed to being the best he can be especially by seeking the advice of other more experienced people. Such curious people always triumph in the end.

This quality is indispensable, to succeed in Business.

There is great good when we learn from the testimony of other people. We save ourselves years of needless mistakes. We learn from people who rose from nothing to something. This is what this book is all about. It is a combination of principles developed from an interview with one of the nation's greatest entrepreneurs. It is a book to obtain for your friends and loved ones. A book that opens you up to wisdom gained from decades of experience of doing the business big time.

Now you sit tight, fasten your belts and let us enjoy the ride. Let the story inspire you.

Indeed, no Business Fails.

My name is "Sreekumar Vadakkeppat", the scenery of "Where I grew up" has been an invaluable energizer in my entrepreneurial journey. It helped me recognize my roots. This knowledge has provided the needed motivation in the face of entrepreneurial challenge.

Growing up in Palakkad, Kerala State in India was everything – the circumstances that characterized my growing up was enough motivation to make a difference.

"When I lost my job and money…, I had no other option of going for a job again. But, while trying applications for the job, a realization tweaked within me and got in touch my highest level consciousness which made me start a business even though I did not know what business to start with! Also, my past experience in coaching brought me here and gave me the confidence to jump in, to launch into the deep".

"Yes, my previous experience in coaching, gave me the needed confidence to walk through an unfamiliar path".

I have been coaching people since 2004, little wonder it did the magic of giving me the needed confidence when it mattered the most. This helps the entrepreneur locate his position on the map early enough with respect to his aspiration. This way you know the dynamics to employ per time to aid your motion. The rule of thumb here, the earlier you start, the better.

YOU ARE UNIQUE

What are you passionate about? If you have not figured this out yet, you should do so right away. To stay really long in business at the top, your business should be centered around your passion. "I am passionate about coaching and having powerful conversations with people, this passion of mine sees to it that I make the news having those conversations"

I was once asked, "What I liked the most about School", with no hesitation I retorted "Freedom" – Now you know where my drive to be financially free comes from. This can be the answer you`ve been looking for, ask yourself the same question. What is that one thing you like the most about school?

There are images in your head, never surrender them for anything in the world.
If I surrendered my visions, I wouldn't be where I am today.

Nothing just happens, "I used to volunteer at Landmark Education as a Head Coach in their Leadership Programs". My passion still found expression in my volunteering. An overnight success would be the longest night of a person`s life. The principle hasn't changed, still no shortcuts to the top.

We need to understand who we are to truly unwind. Unwinding should help us get refreshed and re-energized for a fresh task. What if all the rest you`ve been observing isn't your kind of unwinding? This can be the reason you are always depressed.

For me during my weekends, which basically constitutes my free time, I am either with my family in the house or in an outing with family or yet conducting my Coaching Program.

One thing relaxation should give you is higher productivity, if that is not the case, then probably you haven't identified those activities that help you unwind.

PHILOSOPHY OF LIFE

"There is a great blessing in giving back to humanity", it`s still a mystery. Have you ever wondered why it is entrepreneurs who give the most to the charity whose names occupy the list of the world`s richest for decades! Really, why?

One thing that is common to these individuals is - their giving to charity organizations. They give big time to non-profits.

For me, "I love to support the Start-up Business Stakeholders. I do offer free coaching for them when I see that they are committed yet there is something in their way of being successful". Truth be told, Money is not everything.

You might have heard enthusiastic speakers sound like everyone should be in business; it`s not entirely true. Know your rhythm, identify what gives you fulfillment. I was fortunate to identify mine early as coaching - The present job as a Business Coach to transform an organization by coaching stakeholders (Business Owner / CEO) of the company.

I believe that death is not the end, rather a part of a long journey, a sojourn of attaining the highest level of consciousness. Death is the next door to something greater. What this does to me is that – it helps me make a sound judgment about any action I am to take. I recognize that even beyond here, I will account for my actions, it affects how I do business. It will do the same for you "

The truth is, these questions do not only reveal who I am, they tell a lot about my business.

INFLUENCES THAT MADE YOU

Life is not a vacuum, we are all a product of a combination of some factors. Identifying "Influences" that have contributed to who you are or who you are becoming - is a fast track to correcting such influences if they are negative. However, if they are positive, I say congratulations. Identifying these Influences will help you promote them the more when they are positive. You are able to cultivate them the more.

For me, I could identify three Influences basically, namely" Individual Influences": these people helped me in no little way, while discovering myself early in life. They were: my first standard class teacher for her love and care (Nabeeza Teacher), my 2nd standard class teacher for being there, my awesome 4th standard class teacher, Saraswathi Teacher, for her determination and direction a lot of times, my 9th standard class teacher, Rathnam Teacher, for her 'clarity of thought'. Also my amiable, high-school Mathematics Teacher for his commitment and in-depth knowledge, he helped me pass Mathematics, now I know there is nothing I cannot learn if I will give it the right attention.

Environmental Influences: The toughness attached to the learning environment, helped me develop a great sense of independence, which has been invaluable for me in business. You know someone once said – tough times never last but tough people do. That`s what a tough environment does to you, it gives you elasticity. It did just that to me. With elasticity, you can maneuver your through any challenge

Career Influences: My Degree in Bachelor of Economics has indeed been a blessing. It has complemented my business knowledge tremendously. Fortunately, academically I was an excellent student. I was in the top two in my class during my school days. I wanted to be the "number one" but couldn't do much to get that place. That made me to even think that I was mediocre though I was scoring good marks. You know what it did to me? It fuelled my determination to be the best at whatever vocation I chose in life.

Guess what? I became the number one in college in the final year Degree Results.

Also, I have enjoyed immense mentorship in my career. The people who have mentored me in my career are all my superiors. They are Mahesh Namibiar (Landmark Forum Leader) and

Poornima Nambiar (Landmark Centre Manager). I am eternally grateful for these relationships.

You should also look inward, there are influences attached to your life – unmask them.

YOUR VIEW ABOUT FAMILY

Family is power. Family is a Fortress. Giving all to the family gives me power too. There is pleasure in the family. Ensuring an ideal family enables every member to influence others positively, contribute to others and also affect the society positively too.

This is really important. Even when it appeared that I lost everything; this kept me going still. I was always thinking, "even if you failed multiple times, this time around, succeed for the family – your ever supportive wife, your wonderful daughter". It was indeed igniting and reviving. All of a sudden, energy would surge into from nowhere. I, in turn, confronted my challenge with renewed strength.

I am married to Anithadevi, the woman of my dreams – she is the definition of the ideal partner. She maintains the home front while I face the business battles. She is indeed a pillar of support, my best friend.

With her marriage is bliss. It has been a great honor walking this path with her. She makes marriage easy.

We have one child, a daughter, whose name is ANJALI who is 19 years of age now. With her advent, our life became meaningful. She gives us happy and excitement throughout since her birth!

Our goal as her parent is to help her maximize her highest level of potential, helping her excel in the career she chooses as well as helping her become the ideal woman in her generation. The woman of dignity, poise and great intellectual prowess, who will, in turn, do her husband and family proud.

The family boosts your self-esteem – The right kind of family setting. No matter what, we should reciprocate the unconditional love shown us by family members.

The feeling of fear exists in every single person; every one of us must feel secure. A family will provide one with that security and protection.

My parents are the first two individual who influenced and molded me to become whom I am today. Also my grandmother who had an important role to pull me out of myself. They made me learn what is love and integrity in life and the importance of it in leading a powerful life. Without my father, I don't think I would have learned about integrity so deep. He had shown me given me the courage to be in integrity in life.

Here is what someone says about family - "Happiness is having a large, loving, caring, close-knit family…"

The right orientation about family is of utmost importance.
WHAT DOES HAPPINESS MEAN TO YOU?

To me, Happiness is an uncommon experience where in one feels the positive within oneself. It is a choice one should always make. I believe the source of happiness - is being peaceful and do your best daily to see more good in the world. Happiness comes from achieving a dream and accomplishing a set goal or objective.

Happiness results when we feel satisfied and fulfilled. Happiness is that state of contentment, the feeling that" life is going the way I want it to go".

This state is not exclusive, it is not hard to achieve, and not hard to maintain if you will choose to do so. Embrace the limitless horizon of happiness and dump the despair of depression. It is all a matter of your choice. Which will you choose?

My best job experience was the time I enjoyed my job the most. It was a period when I was working as a Statistician at an Electronics company. The thought of it always inspires me and makes me happy.

My greatest accomplishment is being a Business Coach and being successful as a business coach. They are two different things. A business coach is successful, not when he makes more money, but when his clients are able to do what they really want to do and achieve what they want to achieve – when they are able to turn their intangible dreams into tangibility.

What is your own definition? What do you mean when you say you are happy? To you, Happiness can result when you have all of your needs satisfied. Whatever your definition is, you can choose to be happy.

The story of Helen Keller will always be an inspiring one. She went on to be a university professor despite being deaf and dumb. If she had been bitter and depressed we know there was no way she would have attained that. That is what being happy can do to you.

It helps you make the most of every situation.

CONCLUSION

Whatsoever it is that you do, you can turn Failure into Success. In life, in Business, in your vocation, you can turn the tables.

"It's fine to celebrate success, but it is more important to heed the lessons..." says Bill Gates, the world's richest man.

We do praise those who have triumphed. We do not examine all the times the triumphant have had to learn, unlearn and relearn, hence turning their "luck" around.

In the real sense, No Business Fails, there is only the art of the comeback – The Bounce back. Every seeming failure is a pedestal to achieve more than we had ever imagined. We can BOUNCE back! Sometimes you may need to bounce into something different, that's why there is the need for re-evaluation, re-questioning. We know you had asked the right questions, we are just not sure you provided the right answers. The uncomfortable terrain of life may at times be leading you to where you need to be. It only means there is the need for re-evaluation, the need to sometimes ask the questions perhaps we have not been asking.

There are no Business Failures, only a new opportunity, to ask questions, a chance to unravel our originality like we have never discovered, another time to look in the mirror and ask the ancient question – Who am I?

It's important not to get confused by jargon when trying to navigate the various processes and procedures involved with re-evaluation. When you're exploring concerns regarding life's processes, business strategic processes, we can touch treasures like we have never done before. We can reach gold or even diamond.

When you self-assess, you become an active participant in your own evaluation. Your involvement enables you to honestly assess your uniqueness, strengths and also areas you need to improve. You then can participate more constructively in the evaluation.

Self-evaluation also serves to improve our commitment to goals setting/achievement, personal development, career development and Business development.

This message and lesson are of utmost importance in our personal lives. Many times we get stuck in the traditional cycle and that's where we stay. We are in a hurry, like everyone else yet we make no progress. We get too comfortable that we don't shift our lives from that spot. We become complacent, not realizing, the problem is more of internal than external.

Don't get stuck running the race of life, it is time to look inwards and re-evaluate.

The fast lane or the freeway experience becomes our regular experience, our speed becomes our everyday testimony because we have straightened every lingering internal controversy. There are unlimited benefits when we reassess our lives or redirect our lives. The truth is that a lot of us are afraid in many cases because we don't know what the turnout is going to be like. What hard decisions we might eventually need to make. But it is all worth it. There will there be less stress and fewer uncertainties in our lives.

The promising way out of the chaos we are in right now is to Re-evaluate. Do you want to be sure you need to look inward? I tell you - JUST DO IT! Re-evaluate. Then you realize no Business really fails.

Name	: SREEKUMAR V
Born date	: 24th January 1966
Commitment I have	: Organization Transformation
Actions I do for Performance	: Enlightening People; Establishing
Education I have	: BA, MA, LL B, DBM, PGDPM, PGDOM
Specialized education in	: Ontology, NLP, Handwriting Analysis
Certificates I have	: Certified Business Coach & Certified Goal Attainment Coach
Business I am in	: Business Coaching for business stakeholders
The game I am in	: How to double the business turnover in six months without adding any resources?

MORE ABOUT ME; KNOW ABOUT ME!

At one point of time in my life, I strongly believed that business was not my cup of tea! I thought I was not born for that! They are different breed! I was clear that it is not easy to do business; rather, it is better to work. I did my Post Graduation in Economics, Graduation in Law and few professional PG Diplomas too. I had even 20+ years corporate experience in various fields too as my strength to start a business. But nothing helped me to be successful in business. In fact, when I looked back the two decade corporate experience was better than my entrepreneurial journey! However, after interacting with many entrepreneurs I asked myself "why people have to do business at the cost of their own family, happiness and peace of mind?" That question enabled me to take a U-Turn again and restarted the entrepreneurial journey with a research mind. From then onwards, in my life, the breakdowns gave the way for breakthroughs and miracles! I could turn around my earnings from zero to lacs in the first few months itself! First time I learned in my life that there was something more than the knowledge that creates success in life. Then the journey paved the way for me to discover and create the 'X-SENSE Result Coaching' for Business Stakeholders. It was first applied to various aspects of my life, both personal and business related. I was applying the same to many of my friends and clients to turn around their life and business so as to be more effective, productive, happy and peaceful. That is the space and time the X-SENSE Coaching Design got evolved and I became a 'recommended' Life Coach with a commitment on Business Stakeholders. Now, looking at the kind of breakthroughs 'my people' have, I think that I would have done this at least 15 years back! It is my privilege that I am their Coach and they are very generous to listen to me!

X-SENSE RESULT COACHING

X – SENSE Result Coaching is delivered as a series of Leadership Coaching & Mentoring sessions as well as Group Coaching Programs, mainly confidential in nature. It is a process to create excellence in life. It is beyond the usual improvement and betterment. In this process one would be asking questions themselves which they never asked and find answers in their own way, all to unearth the buried barriers and generate whole new perspectives to achieve what they want to create in life. X – SENSE Result Coaching engagement would enable the organization to have 'High Voltage Performance' and extraordinary business growth with an added benefit of having personal breakthroughs and fulfillment in life itself.

THE KIND OF RESULTS HAPPENED THROUGH X-SENSE RESULT COACHING:
119% increase in business turnover in 7 months time
Became a Global Organization in 8 months
Doubled sales turnover in 32 days
60% increase in sales in four months
9000% ROI in seven months
And the like...

KNOW THROUGH SOCIAL MEDIA CONNECTS AT
https://www.facebook.com/sreekumarvadakkeppat
https://www.facebook.com/XSenseResultCoachings/
https://www.linkedin.com/in/resultcoach/
https://twitter.com/resultcoaches

GAMES I AM UPTO WITH STAKEHOLDERS
Doubling the Business Turnover that one may think not workable / possible
Improve the profitability and productivity
Creating 'high voltage performance'

KNOW MORE VIRTUALLY AT
Website: www.result-coach.com
Email: Sreekumarv24@gmail.com&Sreekumar@result-coach.com
Phone: +91 9845823272

5

THE JOURNEY TO ACHIEVEMENT ...FROM REFUGEE TO RENAISSANCE WOMAN

DR. EMILY LETRAN, BUSINESS COACH, SPEAKER, TRAINER & AUTHOR

I was born in Viet Nam, a war torn country, in the late 1960's. Growing up, what I watched on TV every night were horrific images of the war: bombings of cities and villages, dead bodies and massacre, people fleeing homes and running for bomb shelters. I was lucky enough to grow up in Saigon, the central city of South Viet Nam, and was sheltered with family love. Both of my parents were philosophy teachers who taught the four of us children to be respectful, thoughtful, and responsible.

In April 1975, the war ended. The Americans left Saigon, and that began a series of very dark years. There was a lot of propaganda, from weekly neighborhood meetings to mandatory club for students. There was a shortage of foods and long lines waiting to buy whatever was made available by the government. People changed their outlook in lives. The future was uncertain.

Amidst all those changes, my mother passed away due to cancer. I was 8 years old. Although I had an older brother, I became the "big sister" of the family. I used to run errands across town on a small bicycle, sometimes late at night. I stood in long lines to buy food for the family. Several years later, when my aunt decided to leave the country to avoid the draft in the impending wars with China in the North and Cambodia in the West, my dad told me I would need to leave with her to help take care of several kids, 4 cousins and my brother. So I left with my aunt, and I never saw my dad again. I was 13.

Imagine being on a fishing boat with 60 human beings crammed together like sardines and going for 7 days in the middle of the ocean with very little food and water. Imagine living in a refugee camp, surrounded with stories of pirates, rape, death, and hopelessness for several months, with limited food, water, and electricity. Imagine coming to a foreign country as a refugee, one of those "boat people," without parents and not speaking the language. Imagine sleeping on the floor for several years, winter or summer, because there were 10 people sharing a 2-bedroom apartment. I had been through all that as a refugee from Viet Nam.

When I came to the US, my only luggage was HOPE and FAITH. I stayed up late every night to translate almost every word from English to Vietnamese to learn what was taught in school. For several years, I woke up early every morning to deliver the newspaper on my bicycle, rain or shine. In high school, I would ignore all the parties my friends talked about simply because I did not have nice clothes to wear. The challenges I faced made me stronger. Throughout those early years and all the way to college, I never lost sight of my goal: I wanted to have a professional career where my status and my income would make my family proud, and I studied very hard to achieve that goal. I completed my undergraduate degree in 3 years instead of 4 and completed a Master's Degree at the same time as my dental degree.

As I finished my educational journey, I was really focused to excel in my career. I bought my first dental practice, my second dental practice, then my third dental practice. I got married and had three beautiful children. Life was happy and hectic, until one day my oldest daughter reminded me that I had missed her classroom music recital 4 years before! This was a turning point in my professional career. I realized life was made of precious little moments that we must cherish. I decided to commit and devote time, money, effort into learning the most efficient way to work, implementing the best strategies to manage time, and prioritizing personal life over business life.

Having managed three dental practices at a time and owning multiple commercial buildings for my business, I have learned to systemize business and delegate projects to my team in the most effective way. My love for reading and my thirst for knowledge had led me to attend many business conferences, learning about personal development, business marketing, community service, etc. and 2 years ago, I decided to devote my time to helping business professionals and entrepreneurs maximize their potential, streamline business and increase profits so they can win back time from work for their family and live the best version of themselves. With the training at High-Performance Academy, I shared with my clients the habits that help a person live a joyful, engaged, and fulfilled life.

I believe we are put on this earth for a purpose and we should fulfill our God given potential. Achieving more in life can mean different things to different people.

For me, achieving more means several specific things:
- Having more clarity, confidence, and courage to step into your power, doing what you want to do
- Having more time and energy for yourself, your family, your friends, so you can spread your love and compassion
- Having more influence and success, so you can create more social impact, whether it is building a larger business, creating more jobs or contributing to charities.

It is important for me to help others achieve more in life because I feel we would have a better society if each person is living a better life, maximizing his or her potential, and contributing more to each other. Because I have done it and am a living proof of the process, I teach my clients on High Performance, focusing on CLARITY, ENERGY, PRODUCTIVITY, COURAGE, and INFLUENCE, to transform their daily lives and make a difference in the lives of others.

All of us lead busy lives. Many of my clients wear several hats, as a spouse, a parent, a CEO, or a community leader. They tend to be overwhelmed, stressed, not having enough time trying to do it all. I often remind my clients of their past achievements, to appreciate what they have now, and develop the courage to step into their power, accelerating to the next level.

My clients love my sense of sarcastic humor and the insights I provide them from the 24+ years of experience in the business. They often tell me that they look forward to the coaching call, that they feel more clear after each session with worksheet and action steps recommendation to follow, and that they enjoy my thought provoking, "difficult" questions that challenge their thinking and perspective to the next level. Sometimes the clients just appreciate me listening without judgment, and I help them reframe their focus into a more positive state of emotion.

Imagine how you all drive on the road with a GPS leading from home to your desired destination. Now, pause, take a moment and think, where is the GPS for your life? For your business? Living a high-performance life means living with intentions, knowing what is most important, knowing what will produce results, and knowing what will distract you! I am blessed to be helping business professionals and entrepreneurs maximize their potential and being the best version of themselves.

Imagine going to work and things are in order, so you do not have to worry about all the details.

Imagine coming home after a whole workday still full of energy so you can have a meaningful conversation with your spouse and fun time with your kids.

Imagine being very clear in what you want to achieve and continuously reach milestones of success.

Imagine having someone "got your back" and support you as you take on new projects and venture into unknown territory.

As a High-Performance Coach, I help you make your imagination a reality. When we have a strong desire to succeed and the energy to do it, the sky is really the limit.

I love seeing my client's success because I realize the ripple effect of being a high performer. High performers challenge the status quo. They create social impact and support causes bigger than themselves. Often, they step up into their power because they accept responsibility and roles that are out of their comfort zone. As I work with my client, I am able to help leverage their strengths and improve on their weaknesses. My clients often leave a coaching session feeling empowered, excited, and ready to serve!

My joy of being a dentist, High-Performance Coach, and business strategist is only part of the driving force in my life. I truly love being a philanthropist and had made short term and long-term goals to give back to the communities locally and globally. I feel blessed to be able to start my life in this country many years ago with all the government help and had made a promise to myself to give back whenever I can. My philanthropic journey started with helping patients in my practice, holding community events to give back and extend globally to participating in the mission, establishing my own non-profit, and utilizing my expertise to inspire other professionals to action.

The ultimate joy I have is to spend time with my three children. We cherish our time together walking on the beach, visiting museums and historical sites, browsing specialty shops, laughing over ice cream or boba, and savoring spicy crispy popcorn chicken. While having fun, my children understand my legacy to always show appreciation, to give back, and be a role model for people around me and for generations to come.

One of my greatest joy to give back is to have my Foundation, www.SmileChampions.org, where I provide free basic dental care to veterans and families of disadvantaged background and free business coaching to entrepreneurs who need help getting their business started. I want to help the veterans because they give the most, their own lives, and sometimes receive the least and because I actually end up living in the US as a consequence of the war. I love helping struggling families because I had been there, were going to a restaurant is a luxury, shopping at the mall is a dream, and getting stranded in an old car is a regular occurrence. I understand that sometimes we may not ask for help in tough times, and the fact that someone just voluntarily offers help without expecting anything in return is the greatest gift we can receive.

Once in a while, I would ask the guest on my radio show, "200 years from now, how would you like the world to remember you?" This question at times has brought guests to tears, realizing the legacy they are creating and leaving behind, or maybe they have none at all at the time of the interview. For me, I want people to remember Emily Letran as a philanthropist who brought joy and practical solutions to serve the world.

Every one of us has a story, uniquely ours. Our lives are in turmoil at times, whether we choose to share it or not. I laugh when I hear the statement, "I am held together by duck tape"! If that is the case, let's not allow that by intentions. We should live our lives every day with the understanding that we are responsible for our own joy, our own failures, our own success, and certainly our own emotions. Life happens FOR us, not to us, so that we may learn to be stronger in tough times, not repeating the same mistakes hopefully, and constantly looking for the next peak of achievement, to make a difference in the world with our own personal touch.

Ralph Waldo Emerson says, "What lies behind us and what lies before us are tiny matters compared to what lies within us." We need to awaken that giant within us, living life to its fullest potential, showing appreciation to others to create a world of love and making our dreams a reality by giving 100% effort of ourselves.

Let's write our life story in such a way that when we get to the end, we have only joy and fond memories and no regrets. I truly believe that with a high-performance life, we can all achieve that, and it is my mission to spread the message, teach the concepts and strategies, and transform as many lives as I can as I go on my journey. I invite you to learn more about High Performance, challenge yourself to be better today than yesterday, be successful in all your endeavors, and create a legacy for generations to follow and be inspired.

Dr. Emily Letran D.D.S. M.S.

UCLA Dental School, 1993 (D.D.S. and M.S., Oral Biology)
Certified High Performance Coach (High Performance Academy)
Featured in Dental Town, March 2016, May 2016 (largest international publication for dentists) and Global Women Magazine, UK
Dental Town Mentor for new dentists
Author, "From Refugee to Renaissance Woman," 2014, foreword by David T. Fagan
"Commit to Embracing Your Big Life," 2015, foreword by Sharon Lechter
"Keep Smiling, Shift Happens," 2016
TEDx Speaker, Walnut, California, February 2016
California Women Conference Speaker, May 2017
Migrant Women Conference, UK, May 2017
Smiles At Sea, Cancun, July 2017
Women in Automotive Conference, Orlando, August 2017
10x Wealth and Business Conference, India, September 2017

Dr. Emily Letran is a general dentist who owns two multi-specialty group practices in Southern California. She received her Bachelor of Science in Biology from UC Riverside (magna cum laude, Phi Beta Kappa) in three years. She is a graduate of UCLA School of Dentistry (Dean's Apollonian Scholarship) and received her Master of Science in Oral Biology from UCLA at the same time in four years.

As a mother of three, Dr. Letran creatively balances work, family life, after-school life and her personal life as a growing entrepreneur. She continuously takes courses in clinical dentistry, practice management and marketing, attending multiple business forums to improve her skills to better serve her clients.

Dr Letran is the author of several books. She is also a Certified High Performance Coach, dedicated in helping business professionals maximize their potential in personal and business life, streamline business and increase profits, winning back time from work so they can enjoy that time with their family, children and pursue their passion.

Dr. Letran is the founder of The Emily Letran Foundation, dedicated to providing basic dental care to veterans and families of disadvantaged background in her monthly Free Dentistry Day. Her Foundation is raising funds to attain a mobile dental unit where she can carry her services to outreached communities. The Foundation will also provide scholarships for high performance coaching to help business owners from disadvantaged background get a jump start in growing and accelerating their businesses.

Topics Dr. Emily Letran can speak about:

FAST TRACK TO HIGH PERFORMANCE

ACTION to WINS

Team Building Essentials

Email: emily@exceptionalleverage.com
Cell: 626-808-5762

FREE GIFT:
www.exceptionalleverage.com/ebook
Connect for FREE 30 minutes consultation
www.exceptionalleverage.com/form
www.DrEmilyLetran.com
Follow on Facebook
www.facebook.com/coachemilyletran
Connect on LinkedIn
 https://www.linkedin.com/in/coachemilyletran

Subscribe to podcast
https://itunes.apple.com/ai/podcast/your-life-business-fast-track/id1105004842

STARDOM BOOKS

6

IF YOU THINK YOU CAN ..YOU WILL
- SHEKHAR VIJAYAN, WRITER, MOTIVATIONAL SPEAKER, ACTOR AND A STAND-UP COMEDIAN

I believe that the world will always get what you want if you strive hard for it with complete honesty and passion. I always wanted to be the master of my destiny and I guess the universe too made sure my wish was its command. I am an international entertainer/actor/standup comedian/motivational speaker/fitness expert and a writer. I love the thrill and buzz of entertaining people. I love interacting with people of all age groups and sizes across all genres.

I have the innate ability to make people feel very comfortable with me, trusting in me, confiding in me as I don't judge them. My clients love the charm, passion, presence of mind and honesty I bring to the fore as an entertainer. I have worked with everyone from leading authors like Jeffrey Archer to leading sportsmen like Virat Kohli who are at the top of their game –in entertaining at events. I am also a motivational speaker who inspires everyone with my weight loss story. I have no fear and I have fought the battle of the bulge losing 40 kilos in a year from 125 kilos to 80 kilos and from 46 inches to 32 inches without going to the gym, avoiding everything in white and in a packet

I am passionate about living in the moment, not the past or the future as I feel this very moment defines life. I really enjoy entertaining and inspiring people around me with my contagious enthusiasm and cheer. I am excited about the smiles I can generate. I don't consider my work as an occupation ,I can honestly say I am living my dream. My favorite way to spend a weekend would be starting the day with a 15 km run with my dog, learning some new tricks from her and writing about anything my overactive imagination can fancy during the afternoon.

I have been pursuing my passion as an entertainer for the last couple of years.

I am a Malayalee by birth, I was born and brought up in Delhi and now I live in Bangalore with my wife and my best friend – my golden retriever. I have been here in Bangalore city for the last 17 years. I love Bangalore for its cosmopolitan nature and climate and nothing comes close to this beautiful city.

I do a lot of volunteer activities for my best clients – dogs and for CRYIndia as I love the energy they exude. I Love the CryIndia foundation for the stellar work they do in terms of Child Rights and You. I have won awards of all kinds and of every nature whilst working in the corporate sector but the best award for me is the smile I see on either a small child, girl or an elderly gent's face after I entertain at an event. It would be impossible for me to give up my run in the morning, which is a far cry from what I was a year ago, and my love for eggs. I would like to be remembered as someone who energized and spread love, cheer, and laughter wherever he went as an entertainer.

As a child, I was practically scared of talking and expressing myself. My idea of fun was drawing a landscape painting and watching it till the cows come home. I did not utter a single word till the age of 3 which scared my mom to bits, I was scared of heights and water and I used to make a trip to Mumbai every year to watch the beach there whilst my cousins would frolic in the water, I would just watch by the shore. In the last couple of years, there has been a total turn around. I can charm anyone and everyone around me through the powers of communication. I have overcome the fear of water and height by just trusting Mother Nature and myself much more. I have learned acting, performed in two plays to a capacity crowd killing the perception that you need to show your talent at a young age. Age is just a number and if you have the ability, focus, and passion you will drive your way through any wall.

I strongly believe in the powers of all modes of communication and I got a taste of it when I was a tiny toddler and at that impressionable age, some images and moments just stick. I had an aunt who had a persona, which was very dominating, and she was a wonderful storyteller and one fine night when I was spending my summer vacations on a particularly hot day in Kerala, she came in and showed me the power of storytelling. She had recently watched the south Indian movie – Manichitrathazhu on the big screen and in the middle of the night she had come to the home to tell us what the movie was about. The village where I was staying suffered frequent power cuts and the voltage was at an all-time low, you could practically see the light just flicker away. My Aunt dressed in a beautiful red saree seated herself in a comfortable position making sure everyone around could hear as well as see her well. The way she recounted the story of this supernatural film with all the sound effects, the imagery was a sight to behold and that's when I got hooked on the power of storytelling, which can be really engaging.

My mom was my most influential person for me whilst I was growing up as a kid, she stood by me through thick and thin. I was not a particularly intelligent student and she took things up for me when I was bullied in school. She is extremely modern and independent in her thought process and she allowed me to bloom in only the way I can

I loved history because somewhere they were all wonderful stories, which mixed facts with fiction. My history teacher had proclaimed that I would make history in a sarcastic manner when I had fared very badly in history in the pre-boards. I did take it as a challenge and scored really well in the history subject in my tenth standard boards, making the history teacher eat her words literally. I was not very fond of any of my teachers as I felt they were not sensitive enough and were more concerned about rankings and the students who showed better attention levels in a class. As a student I was inactive socially and academically, I did not participate in any forum as I was painfully very shy.

My favorite sport was cricket and lawn tennis and liked the poetry in them. I loved the way the mind and body had to work in synch in both these sports which used different skill sets and got maximum results.

I was inspired by Mohammed Ali and Michael Jackson as they were entertainers from the word go. Ali in the boxing ring and Michael Jackson for the way he used to just weave all the elements of entertainment when he performed.

My first job and worst job was as a system admin for a bank in Bangalore where my colleagues hated my guts and the CEO of the company had a tongue, which was filthier than a sailor docking at various ports. I hated every moment of this experience as everything in this company was about the CEO who was like a one-man army and he could literally arm twist his way to get his work done. I decided that I could not work in such a stifling environment and in a skip level meeting I voiced the problems everyone faced and moved onto a call center for a leading computer manufacturing company which was setting up operations in Bangalore for the first time. My ideal job is right now when I am living my dream, traveling around the world entertaining people across all corners, spreading fun, cheer and laughter whilst also ensuring I am honest and true to myself

We did have a baby girl last year and we had named her Akira which in Japanese means the brave warrior, she was a preterm baby who lived every day like her last day for three months , she was a fighter and she was with us for three months till she decided that she needs to go to a better place . The passing away of my baby girl taught me a lot of things – brought me closer to my brave wife – one for all, all for one, life is meant to be lived in the present, birth and death are the only permanent touch points in life and everything else is complementary. As a parent, I would be the coolest dad as I love interacting with kids and I do believe there is a sense of fun and impishness in whatever I do. I don't have a goal as a parent, I just want my kids to have their own journey because we all have our own paths which we follow seeking peace, fun, cheer, laughter, and happiness out of it

I have read about the world wars, the Indian freedom struggle but for me whilst growing up the war which shaped me in a certain way was the Kargil war ,the bravery displayed by our soldiers whilst guarding the borders making sure the Indian Flag flies high at all time was goose bump-inducing almost prompting me to join the army. I would have loved to meet Martin Luther King and Mahatma Gandhi as they were inspirational in their own right galvanizing people around them because of the power of their thoughts

Every traveling experience of mine has been memorable and I would recommend everyone to travel far and wide see the world, experience its flavors in its entirety. I loved the trip I made to Sydney, Australia when I was invited to entertain at an event for the Indian community .the Amphitheater, where I was entertaining, was the same performance venue which says a footfall of close to fifty thousand people where the legendary Michael Jackson had performed which was a huge moment for me . I also had an opportunity to make a trip to the beautiful as well as terrifying Mount Kailash and the ethereal Manasarovar Lake and I had a near-death experience there where I experienced an external source which guided me through the whole journey when I was almost about to blackout at the highest point in Mt Kailash called the Drolma La Pass where a butterfly guided me through the rest of the journey. The dip in Manasarovar Lake will make you go through a plethora of emotions and at that lake, I just cried.

When was the last time you had gone to drop your mother in law to the railway station and you end up traveling practically the entire distance with her because of certain forces of nature and time? My mother in law was travelling by the Shatabdi express and I like a dutiful son in law made sure we reached well in time in the railway station , carrying her bags to her seat and whilst I was about to disembark , the compartment doors were locked and there were people ahead and behind me who had no inclination of giving way and by the time I reached the compartment door which was locked airtight , the train picked up speed and the platform was nowhere in sight ..before I could say Jai Mata Di everyone in the compartment had settled in with their papers and coffee whilst I was thinking how do I jump out of train which is cruising at 81mph and the next station where the super fast Shatabdi Express would stop as an afterthought was at Katpadi Junction which was close to 108kms to Chennai , As soon as the train stopped at this station I jumped out, adjusting my shorts, running faster than Usain Bolt to the ticket counter, bought return tickets for a train which was returning back to Bangalore and thought of the six hours I spend in almost travelling all the way to Chennai which was an embarrassing and a funny experience

My happiest memory are many but if I have to single out a couple of instances – that moment when I skydived at the beautiful Queenstown in New Zealand at 15,000 feet, snorkeling in the deep blue waters of Maldives overcoming my fear of water and when my baby daughter was born. These are moments when I cried, smiled and laughed as I felt a sense of fulfillment and calm whilst everything around me was moving forward. Happiness for me is moments which are there in everything and everyone and I strongly believe in the power of doing good and being honest to oneself.

Shekhar Vijayan

I am an entertainer by profession who loves the thrill and the buzz of entertaining people. I am a writer, motivational speaker, actor and a stand-up comedian and I am on social media as
Twitter – Shevititan
Instagram- Shevititan
Snapchat- Shevititan

My website –www.shekharvijayan.com and I am on LinkedIn as ShekharVijayan

My Facebook page - https://www.facebook.com/mcshekharvijayan/ contains details of all the work I do and the videos I share around losing weight and staying fit
My YouTube page
https://www.youtube.com/channel/UCyFf1QtQ6rv1aSvKJSwWfRQ
1) talking about my weight loss journey for a Mumbai based startup focused on showcasing the most powerful " Real Life Stories" -https://www.youtube.com/watch?v=U4ri9vGEMKs
2) as a Youth Icon for a private TV Channel - https://www.youtube.com/watch?v=tx94_ltz4DM
3) talking about fitness and transformation - https://www.youtube.com/watch?v=7Wi_Y0uxUTQ
4) talking about fitness and transformation - https://www.youtube.com/watch?v=FRK10V4voeU
5) myshowreel as an entertainer -

https://www.youtube.com/watch?v=5fwXTLcZpSw
   6) myshowreel as a travel video blogger /influencer-
https://www.youtube.com/watch?v=28dYiiHw07A

I would like to do speaking engagements for individuals, customized groups and corporate and all the details to reach out to me are on www.shekharvijayan.com

7

MY LIFE IS MY MESSAGE
THE JOURNEY TO DISCOVERING LIFE'S PURPOSE
-BY FAYE KITARIEV, OLYMPIC FIGURE SKATING COACH

"THE TWO MOST IMPORTANT DAYS IN YOUR LIFE ARE THE DAY YOU ARE BORN AND THE DAY YOU FIND OUT WHY."

~Mark Twain

Every morning I do my Sadhana, a set of spiritual exercises, which helps me to energize, center, strengthen, and inspire myself. These exercises also contribute to improving my concentration, discipline, and spiritual connection. One of the exercises is reading a passage from an inspirational book. One day, I was reading Wayne Dyer's Power of Intention. A quote got my attention: "You receive what you desire for others." I sat with it for a little while, digesting it, then journaled. Nothing special was happening, except I made a note for myself: "Create a set of affirmative coasters for water to charge water with positive affirmations." The next paragraph in my journal said, "Wrote water affirmations." That's it! I don't remember how exactly I ended up writing the first statement. But I wrote five and cut the paper into five index-sized cards. I then put my water bottle on one of them to charge. I was pleased with myself. I felt that I would finally be able to remember to stay more centered during the day. I had been feeling frustrated with myself for getting distracted all the time by social media, emails, and incoming texts. I needed a different kind of discipline; it felt as if morning Sadhana wasn't enough for the level of mastery I was seeking. Somehow, I wanted my whole day to be like Sadhana: centered, grounded, and connected. As I took a sip of water out of my bottle, which was charging on "I am unlimited abundance I crave," I suddenly had a vision. I could clearly see beautiful coasters with different affirmations helping billions of people to stay more focused, productive, kind, loving, wise, abundant, patient, connected, and healthy. My mind was thinking a million thoughts per second, and within an hour, I wrote fifty statements. These statements were not ordinary affirmations. They were intentions. Affirmations were not enough; they were too passive. To create change, one must take action. To take action, there must be the intention. It was October 3, 2016. I didn't have the slightest idea that it was going to be the day I'd realize my mission on this planet, the day when i'MAGiNTLiFE™ was conceived.

While i'MAGiNTLiFE™ was conceived on October 3, 2016, I've been coaching people since 1990; 27 years, that is.

WHO AM I?

People know me as a coach, author, and speaker. They know me for my passion for unlocking the hidden potential, the greatness that is within every one of us. I did this first as a skating coach, then later as a performance coach. I believe that one of my biggest gifts is the ability to see the unseen capacities within people and the courage to challenge them to bring out more than they believed they could. I help people feel that they have all the resources within themselves to reach their dreams.

When asked what am I most passionate about personally and professionally, it is the same: living an ordinary life in an extraordinary way. Personally, I am passionate about discovering my potential, living my Best Self, being present, and sharing my voice. Professionally, I am passionate about helping others realize their potential, living their Best Selves, being present, and sharing their voice. I am in love with my clients and with witnessing the unfolding of their greatness, the excitement and surprise they feel when they experience the "aha" moments and the joy and fulfillment that come into their lives as they discover their purpose and voice and align with their Best Selves. With the creation of i'MAGiNTLiFE™, I suddenly saw the possibility of making a difference in billions of people's lives. I see i'MAGiNTs™ changing the consciousness of the planet. I see children in schools practicing i'MAGiNTLiFE™ and growing into responsible, loving, kind, patient, respectful, willing, courageous adults. I see heads of the governments drinking i'MAGiNTended™ water and making conscious decisions for the highest good of all of the humanity and our planet. I see a new generation of humans raised with i'MAGiNTs™ living in peace, abundance, and unity, being their Best Selves. Is this my personal or professional vision? It's both. That is all I talk about, and that is all I do with my life. When I am not working, I am networking, taking a power nap, or attending a seminar. Sometimes, I get to see an inspirational movie or live performance. I love Cirque du Soleil. I love seeing people doing seemingly impossible tricks, pushing their creativity to the next levels, performing at their near-the-top capacities. I always look for ways to be inspired. If my week is filled with opportunities to inspire others, then my ideal weekend would be being inspired myself.

FORMATIVE YEARS

I grew up in a Jewish family in Latvia, a former republic of the Soviet Union, a country that doesn't exist anymore. As a young child, I didn't enjoy playing with the kids my age. I always preferred the company of adults or much older children. I also liked to play by myself, cutting small animals out of magazines or reading books. When I was 2.5 years old, my mother took me to the Ice Skating Academy. She dreamed of me becoming a figure skating champion. Unfortunately, I didn't share this dream with her. My early recollection of skating is mental, emotional, and physical abuse. My name was Stupid, Lazy Pig. That's what I was called daily. It wasn't long before they kicked me out of the skating academy to give my spot to a more promising athlete. My mother's relentless commitment to my continuing skating changed the course of my life. One day at the public skating rink, she was approached by a tall stranger pointing in my direction. "This talented, beautiful girl, is that your daughter?" she said. "I am a new coach with the Academy, and I would love to teach your little girl." My new coach, Zhanna, became the most influential person in my childhood and beyond. She was the only person who saw me as beautiful and talented. It was her gift to me and the world to change the way I saw myself and to inspire me to start showing up for my life. Through her loving guidance, I became the State Champion. Winning the State Championship had a significant impact on my life. I realized that I had the potential to me and that everyone had that potential—every single one of us. Realizing this Potential within myself and others became the mission and purpose of my life. This is why I became a coach, speaker, author and the creator of i'MAGiNTLiFE™. This is why I dedicated my life to studying, implementing, and developing the tools and strategies of life mastery - to inspire, empower and teach people these tools - so that we can break free from self-imposed limitations to enjoy fulfilling meaningful lives, realize our dreams, and inspire others to achieve theirs. In 2014, I was chosen for a Member Moment in the

Toastmasters International Magazine out of 330k members after sharing my story from Stupid, Lazy Pig to State Champion. My real medal turned out to be the opportunity to inspire people through that story over and over again.

After I stopped figure skating, I picked up theater as my extracurricular activity. The acting was one thing I became passionate about in my teen years. I could give up everything to be in rehearsals or performances. There was nothing that I didn't like about acting. I felt that the stage was the only place where I could express myself and share my voice.

My favorite subjects in school were history and math. However, to be honest, I didn't like school. The Soviet school was like a military boot camp, where everyone had to be the same, think the same, and look the same. I guess I was oppositional defiant and never missed an opportunity to express my liberal nature. This trait made me popular with few teachers and very unpopular with many. I also had just a handful of friends, didn't have teen-idol, and never participated in the popularity contests. Academically, I was a solid B student, never putting much effort into my studies. I was doing enough just to get by.

People would probably have difficulty believing that as a teen I had very low self-esteem, didn't have any goals, and didn't care about studying. I was also upset a lot. I wrote my first poem when I was 12 and was writing poetry until my early 20s. I also wrote a detective novel when I was 16. I didn't publish it but have several notebooks of my childhood writings still. I think I was depressed, and all of my poems were about sadness or war.

When I was 18 and Gorbachev became the new president, he made it possible for Jews to leave the Soviet Union. My parents took the opportunity to build a new future for our family and to reunite with many of our relatives and friends who defected many years ago. The price for such an opportunity was to give up everything we owned. Within the first couple of weeks of our arrival in the States, I had to get a job to help my family. I never had to work before and was scared. I could barely speak any

English and had no special skills. My very first job was accompanying nurses attending to patients in poor neighborhoods of NYC. I was being paid $4 per hour. I had a fur coat that I brought with me from the Soviet Union. The nurse I was partnering with asked me to get a cheap jacket, as she was worried to go with me into impoverished areas and get attacked. But there was no money to get me another coat.

Thinking of the difficulties we had to endure in the early days of our immigration, I feel grateful for and proud of my parents' courage and faith and their decision to leave. They didn't speak English and didn't have an Ivy League education or highly sought-after skills. They were average people with average IQs. But they made this reckless decision to leave all behind and to become successful in the new country. Their gift was courage and relentless commitment to succeed. Perhaps the world knows much more accomplished people than my parents were, but to me, they were the exact parents I needed to become who I became today.

Coming to the Land of Opportunity at 18 meant getting an education that would offer me a stable and prosperous future doing anything I loved. I decided to go to the University of Delaware to pursue a B.S. in Physical Education with a concentration in Figure Skating Science. U of DE was the only university in the United States where I could receive this degree and become a coach like my Coach Zhanna. It was a wild decision, opposed by most of my family members, but I was stubborn and followed my heart instead. Today, I am so thankful for the wisdom, courage, and intuition of my younger Self. She made choices that set up a platform for me to live the life of my dreams and inspire others to do the same. If I could give her advice, I'd suggest that she add some classes on marketing, advertising, and business development. It could have helped me a lot in my entrepreneurial journey. My younger Self-didn't see herself as a leader of a global consciousness transformation movement such as i'MAGiNTLiFE™. She only saw herself as an Olympic Figure Skating coach at the time. I think she would be happy and proud to find out who she became later.

The biggest influence in my career was a legendary gymnastics coach, Bella Karolyi, who produced over 192 medalists in the Olympics and the World, European, and National Championships. I wanted to emulate him. I saw him speak at a conference, and he was so inspirational that I vowed that one day I'd speak at the conference too and inspire others like he had inspired me. It took me 23 years to do that, but in 2015, I spoke at this conference, presenting a speech called Dreams Do Come True and my bestselling book, Choreography of Awakening.

COACHING SKATING

For over 25 years, I coached competitive figure skating. I believed that I had found my passion for life and knew exactly what I wanted to do and where I wanted to go. I loved helping children discover their gifts, and I loved competitions where we had opportunities to prove to the world that we had the capacity to be and do more than anyone had expected from us. Ultimately, it was my dream to coach at the Winter Olympic Games. Everyone, including my family and friends, told me that it was a crazy goal and that I would burn out and be disappointed because I would spend my life chasing an impossible dream, lose my life and family, and never reach it anyway. My peers didn't tell me that I was crazy. They did everything they could to set up an obstacle course for my students and me en route to this dream. There were days where I was really down, as I felt that this obstacle course was too much to overcome. I cried, felt depressed, refocused, and came back to try once again. Every time I was pushed off, I got back on with a new strategy. Now I can see how much they were helping me. At the time, I thought they were stopping or slowing me down. However, now I can recognize that they were speeding me up, helping me learn, grow, reinvent, and get stronger and more courageous. Today, I can honestly see that i'MAGiNTLiFE™ wouldn't exist without their "help." I am grateful for all of my teachers in disguise.

In 2006, my dream of coaching an Olympic competitor came true. Suddenly, it was no longer a dream. I was training Sasha Cohen, an American favorite, a 21-year-old protégé expected to win the Olympic gold. My opponent-peers turned into friends, and my family bragged about how they helped me. At the time, I thought that I had made it. However, very quickly, I learned that the Olympics wasn't what I wanted or expected. Sasha lost the gold and got silver. I wasn't passionate about being at that competition. My passion was about unlocking one's potential. About discovering one's personal best. I realized that you could be an Olympic silver medalist, one of the best in the world, and still not the best version of yourself: unfulfilled and unhappy. When we live anything less than who we really are, we cannot feel whole and joyous. Finding ways to fulfillment and happiness became my new passion.

AND NOW...

Today, I love leading a community meet-up group called "Make the Impossible Possible," where I share some life mastery tools with people who need help to make a change in their lives. I also speak in schools to inspire children to believe in themselves and to follow their dreams. As i'MAGiNTLiFE™ picks up the momentum, it is my vision to create a non-profit organization for children and teens all over the world to teach them life skills of nonviolent communication, compassion, understanding, forgiveness, and acceptance. In this organization, older children will be learning facilitation skills, and they will be teaching younger kids. They will learn how to operate their minds and how to live in their Best Selves. I believe that children should learn from each other, as they learn more from their peers than from adults.

My role model in life is Gandhi. A quote is etched into the wall of my office: "My life is my message." I want to be remembered in the way Gandhi is remembered. It is a tall order, and living at such high level of integrity and commitment is challenging. I believe that God or the Universe has given me a job to contribute to the evolution of the Universal Consciousness through developing, teaching, and spreading i'MAGiNTLiFE™ globally. It is my responsibility to become a highly tuned instrument, capable and willing to live this mission. It is my wish to be remembered as an "Avatar of Lord's Peace, as Gita's Daughter and Beloved Student."

I have a 16-year-old daughter. My goal as a parent is to be a role model for my daughter to follow her heart, live a life of purpose and meaning, and trust that Spirit has her best interest in mind. As a parent, I hold loving space for her to discover who she is and support her in finding her own path.

I lost both of my parents. While my life wasn't sugarcoated, and I had to fight for the approval and acceptance of my mom and live through episodes of escalated disagreements and arguments then years of healing different issues associated with my upbringing, I wouldn't change anything. Their death, especially my mom's, made me see things in a different light. I learned to see my parents as people with their personal struggles, wounds and wins. I learned to see them through the eyes of love and compassion. If there is anything that I want people to learn, it is to see their parents as Spiritual Beings living through the challenges of human experience and to appreciate that before it is too late. I also learned that my parents are my Angels, and they are here with me and find ways to communicate their presence. This is one of the reasons my publishing company is called Gita's Press. Gita was the auspicious name of my Mother. I realized that I am Gita's Daughter, and as such, I have a special mission to carry forward.

Today it is Charles, my partner, who is my biggest supporter and believer.

If I could live in a different historical era, other than the present, I'd choose to live during Jesus' time because I want to know what was special about him, what exactly was he teaching, how he lived his life, and how he became who he was. And if I had a time machine, I would then move to a time to meet Gautama

Siddhartha. I think we would have a fabulous conversation!

My definition of happiness would be living my life's purpose to the highest potential. Happiness is knowing that I am making a difference in the world. Happiness is being aligned with Higher Power. Happiness is having the energy to give all of myself every day. I must say that I do live in proximity to my definition of happiness.

I don't believe in death. While we shed our bodies, consciousness takes the form of energy. I am not meant to know what that means, yet I do enjoy contemplating it.

While I do not follow any particular religious dogma, I believe that Earth is a school and everyone signs up for their own curriculum. Resolving and clearing this curriculum to realize my Highest Self and the Loving Essence of God is my religion. i'MAGiNTLiFE™ is exactly that.

I learned many lessons in my life and continue learning daily. Perhaps the Law of Reflection is one of the biggest lessons I learned so far. Maybe the day will come when I will be ready to share this lesson in its entirety with the world.

I am an ordinary being, choosing to live an extraordinary life, pushing my limits every day, living what I believe is my mission and purpose. There is no magic in my life, other than that I chose to follow my heart and be present to Divine Guidance that every one of us has.

"WHAT THE OUTSTANDING PERSON DOES, OTHERS WILL TRY TO DO. THE STANDARD SUCH PEOPLE CREATE WILL BE FOLLOWED BY THE WHOLE WORLD."
~Bhagavad Gita.

It is my mission to transform myself into that outstanding person, using i'MAGiNTLiFE™ as a tool, and inspire others to follow in this pursuit. Just imagine what our world could become! Join me on this Path of Transformation!

Faye Kitariev

Faye Kitariev is the Founder, CEO, and creator of i'MAGiNTLiFE™. She is a bestselling author, international speaker, Certified High-Performance Coach, and former Olympic figure skating coach.

After 2006 Winter Olympic Games, where her student captured a Silver medal, Faye turned her attention to performance psychology and why some athletes reach their potential while others fall far short. Her study of personal growth and development led her to fields as diverse as sports and spiritual psychology, yoga, meditation, tai chi, and Aikido. She became obsessed with understanding how the human mind works.

After graduating with a Master of Arts degree in Spiritual Psychology and experiencing profound personal transformation, Faye decided to dedicate her life to studying, implementing, and developing tools for life mastery and to empower, inspire, and teach people these tools so that they can enjoy fulfilling, meaningful lives, realize their dreams, inspire others, and contribute to the evolution of the universal consciousness. It is this mission and almost 30 years of experience, research, and intense daily practice that led Faye to the creation of i'MAGiNTLiFE™.

Faye is passionate about inspiring kids and teens of all ages discover their inner strengths and personal power and make the impossible possible.

To contact Coach Faye visit www.coachfaye.com and www.imagintlife.com

8

JOURNALISM JOURNEY TO BECOMING THE CHIEF OF BUREAU
- BY SEETHALAKSHMI, METRO EDITOR (SENIOR ASSISTANT EDITOR/CHIEF OF NEWS BUREAU) THE TIMES OF INDIA

The first time, I told my grandmother (who is no more now), that I want to be a `news' person, a writer..she scoffed at me: "Writers don't make money. What will you do to earn your daily bread? your parents have educated you not to sit at home" I was in class 9 then -- a 15 year old.

Coming from a 79-year-old, who was a voracious reader, I was stunned. Very politely I told her: ``How are you reading so many books.?. What if each of the writer's grandmother had discouraged him/her? Would you have had the book in your hand today?". She did not have any answers.

Hailing from a traditional Tamil Brahmin family in Kerala,

South India, it was a given for all, to pursue bank jobs and take up the finance route. But in school, my biggest problem was Math. My schoolteachers would often compare me, in the class, with my brothers, who scored centum in Math. My scores would not go beyond 70.

And predictably, all of them chose Commerce streams after class 10, which had Accountancy, and Math. So the only girl child in the family too had to pursue that. But numbers and I were total enemies. I swore I will never do Math, after class 10. And there I was defying the `Tam Bram' culture of not going the Science and Commerce way and choosing Humanities. I chose History, Sociology, Political Science and Psychology.

Not someone to give up. my Mother T V Rajalakshmi was keen, I work in a bank, as it was the most comfortable job for a girl in the 90s. ``You know you will get a bank loan for a house..finish work at 3 pm.. what else does a girl want? She asked.
She persuaded my brother to help me apply for the Banking Services Recruitment Board examinations (BSRB) - an All India entrance examinations for bank jobs. I was totally disinterested in preparing and appearing for the exams. But he did it very diligently.

The elder brother that he was..he duly picked up the form, filled it up and did just about everything that was needed for an entrance examination application. And when the examination day arrived, he promptly dropped me at the bus stop too to head to the examination center. And he left. But I would not board any bus. I just walked back home and told my mother: I don't want to do this examination. I don't like sitting in a place and working. I want to meet people from various sectors and write about them.

There began my journey for Journalism. After class 12 at the Bishop Cottons Girls School in Central Bengaluru, I joined a college, that had Journalism at the under graduation level. I chose Journalism, English Literature and Psychology as my core subjects. My mother began liking my focus. One day she said: "Now that we have allowed you to study and chase your dreams. let's see how successful you will be. I will pray for you."

That set me going. I was not going to fail. Now, that I have rebelled against the traditional Science and Commerce, there was no way I am going to fail.

The next three years of my undergraduate program was hectic. I would sit on the front bench of the Journalism class and take down, every word that the teacher would utter.. My classmates would ask me, why was I so determined to do well. "I told them, I will become a journalist. And I will work hard to achieve that."

Three years passed and I was a graduate now with a degree in Journalism. I went to a newspaper office and asked them if I could work. The curt reply was: "We don't hire freshers.. Get experience and then come." Disappointed I was. But swore that, when I get the experience of working in a newsroom, I will be so excellent in my work, that you will call me.

And that's exactly what happened. Five years after I joined the Times of India - India's largest selling newspaper, I got a call from the editor who asked me to come after I gained experience. I said a firm NO. Here I was working in the leading National daily and making a mark for myself, I would not let go of this.

The journey began in 1994 when I joined TOI as a trainee journalist. The first day at work was a dream come true for me. As I walked into the second floor of SB Towers, MG road and handed in my appointment letter, I could not believe myself. I told myself: ``Here is it is.. I have worked for this. But my real work starts now and how I am going to make use of this golden opportunity of getting my dream job".

The next 15 years was a roller coaster ride. I would breathe work..worked really hard... pushed myself and said: I have to be the best every day... I follow this even to this day when I have completed a good 20 years in this profession, with seven to eight best journalist awards to my credit.

I was very harsh on myself all these years. I would cry when I missed a story to another newspaper. I would punish myself if I slipped up and made mistakes.

I wrote articles/ news stories and features on virtually every sector - from education to infrastructure to Science to crime to health. To my credit today, I have over 4000 articles and 200 columns.

My mother would proudly tell her friends that my daughter is a journalist...and "did you read her article today". This was it. I wanted this moment when she and my father would feel proud of me. What better way of giving back to your parents than making them proud of your achievements.

Of the several awards that I bagged for Excellence in Journalism, the Zee Best Media Promising Journalist award will be etched in my memory, not because it was the first award in my kitty, but because my parents realized that I was on the right path.

On the award day, when I walked up to the dais to receive it, my parents screamed with joy and told everyone around, in the star hotel: That is my daughter.

They say, for a woman to be successful in her career, especially in India, she needs a solid and supportive family. I was blessed with that. Doting parents and brothers, an extremely supportive techie husband V M Sundaram and an even more supportive daughter Aditi, who understood my dreams of making it big in this profession. Not to forget my mentor - the then editor H S Balram, who pushed the envelope for me every day. I owe to him for all the learning.

My first award propelled me to work more and encouraged me to do better. In 2009, The Times of India, which had captured the Bengaluru market was getting competition for the first time in.. A new newspaper was to be launched

The next big thing that came my way, was the nomination by the United States Government for the prestigious International Visitors Leadership Programme (IVLP) in 2010. Five journalists from India were chosen for the scholarship and Lo! I was the only one from South India.

A fully paid scholarship for 21 days and a guest of the United States government. I taped myself and asked if I am really that good!

The other awards came my way. In 2015, I won the Namma Bengaluru Award - for my outstanding contribution to the city of Bengaluru. The heartening part of the award was citizens of Bengaluru voted for me, as the best journalist!

After being a reporter for a good 14 years, I was asked by my editor Mr. Balram, if I am ready to pass on my skills by heading a team. I was reluctant and apprehensive. But went with the confidence that my seniors had in me.

And Lo! in 2016, I won the Best Editor award!

WHAT DID THIS JOB TEACH ME :

Over the years, I realized that every story that I chased, every person, I met was an experience and a learning. Like they say, there is a lesson in everything - good or bad experience..like there is news of every piece of paper. It is for us to find it. And I have hundred such examples. Here are a few that taught me persistence.

One story on starving Sri Lankan refugee children that went global started from a piece of paper, I found on my table.

"on that is housing them have run out of funds...they are in Jakkur in North Bengaluru...."

It was a nameless statement.

Curious.. I dialed the number. An old, frail voice on the other side said: "Come over and meet us".

Not sure if it was someone who was playing a prank, I pondered if I should pursue this... then I decided I must.. I asked for directions and reached the house, off Indiranagar in East Bengaluru. The man (in his early 60s), a Sinhalese by birth, a refugee from Srilanka who had come to the city after fleeing from the strife-torn nation began briefly telling me the story of a refugee home in the city.

I told him.. I have to visit the home and see it for myself before writing anything. I need to meet the refugee children. I insisted I go on my own.

I asked him for the Jakkur refugee home directions and headed there straight to see for myself if all that was on that piece of paper was true!!

In the middle of a huge playground stood a building ..slightly dilapidated.. the paint wearing off. I asked the security for the kitchen. I entered it to find it dark and empty and that too at 9 am. all the stocks in the storeroom were empty. There were a few empty sacks lying around the kitchen..the dusty gas stove had not been lit for weeks now.

Convinced that the starvation story was true. I walked up to the classrooms (the society was running a school for these refugee children on the same campus)..what I saw stays with me even today.. young boys and girls..frail and hungry.. yet were listening in rapt attention to the class teacher... I excused myself and spoke to the teacher to confirm if the starvation angle was indeed true...
she began weeping.. she quickly gestured to the little children (all in the age group of 7 to 13 years) and in minutes they were all around her...Then she told me: "Ask them.. remember children don't lie! Saying that she went away..not wanting to influence their statements to a journalist.

I asked one of them: "What did you eat this morning?" Nothing..he said.. Then I asked him: "Last night?"

"Nothing", came the reply... and yesterday afternoon? Nothing he said: I felt I was choking when I heard him repeat nothing for every question.

By then the other children began talking... in unison, they said: "We have not eaten for five days now...and whenever we are hungry. We open a book and read!!" (That was the headline for my

story.
that hit the front page of The Times of India the next day).

What happened after the story appeared in TOI was mind-boggling. As the largest media house in India, we do not seek funds on behalf of anyone. So there were no numbers that public could call and help. TOI's MG road office was flooded with calls as early as 7 am the next morning (It was January 26... so holiday).

There were five-star hotels, which said they want to start feeding the children from that day, there were families calling in to get the address to take lunch for the children that afternoon. there were corporate houses that called in to say they wanted to meet me to understand how they can support by mobilizing funds.. there were NGOs that rushed to the refugee home to take stock of the children's needs. A Norwegian couple donated two cows for the children's home, two days after the article appeared so that the children can drink milk.

The response stunned me. The electricity Board which had cut off power supply to the refugee home (because they had not paid the bills) restored power supply the day the article appeared. The examination board officials landed at Jakkur to allow the children appear for the examinations (they had refused permission because the examination fees had not been remitted to the board)... water supply was restored.

Since TOI carried the article in its other editions, I began getting calls from other cities where students wanted to pledge their one months; pocket money for the refugee home, embassies which wanted to sponsor meals for the children. We at TOI helped the home open a bank account, so that the funds may be transferred there.

And in 10 days, Rs Eight Lakh was collected. This was beside the contributions in kind which ranged from medicines, blankets, books, and clothes for the refugee children, which had flooded the Jakkur home.

I have always believed that the media is powerful and the pen is mightier than the sword..but this story that won me the European Union Fellowship on Malnutrition strengthened my belief that the print journalism will not die in India, anytime soon.

In the professional circles, I am a journalist known for being persistent. And this quality sometimes could annoy your sources. No one likes to be pushed. Not by a journalist at least. But, I have always earned a good friend, only after an argument with a majority of my sources - who range from Vice-chancellors, ministers, bureaucrats, scientists and experts from various domains.

My argument to get that story out of anyone is very simple. The world must know if you had done well. And if you did something bad, then the world has a right to know, and I as a journalist have the right to ask!

Persistence, courage, happiness, anger management, patience, time management, leadership skills, people management --- this job just opened the world for me at 22, when I joined as a trainee journalist.

Today, when I look back -- from a trainee journalist with a monthly stipend to being the Chief Reporter (City editor) managing the news of 1.1 crore population, I have no regrets of the punishment, I meted out to myself..when I started my journey.

The key, as I tell my team every day is to stay spirited..confident and passionate about what you do.

Seethalakshmi

CURRENT JOB AND DESIGNATION:

Seethalakshmi S
Metro Editor (Senior Assistant Editor/Chief of News Bureau)
The Times of India
Bangalore

As a Metro Editor in the number one English Daily -- The Times of India, I am in charge of newsbreaks for the entire city of Bangalore as also Karnataka state.

* All news bureaus---------Education, health, Science and Technology, Crime, Urban infrastructure/mobility, Aviation/Space, culture/heritage, city civic agencies, environment/wildlife/ecology, urban mobility, women/child welfare, government departments, the high court are handled by me.

* I head a 14-member team of reporters and four photographers/graphic team.

EXPERIENCE:

I have gained tremendous knowledge and confidence in my 17-year experience as a journalist. I started off as a trainee journalist in The Times of India in 1994, where I covered/wrote numerous news reports/features/interviews on virtually every subject listed above. I have spearheaded numerous Times of India (TOI) campaigns for better Bangalore-- civic campaigns, education and health campaigns for the newspaper.
This won me the Namma Bengaluru Award in 2012, where 60,000 Bengalurians voted for me and nominated me for the award.

* For eight years, I covered the government (its various departments and policies).

* I have covered all the general elections (parliamentary elections) and all assembly and civic elections since 1994.
This gave me a great exposure to the working of various governance units at the micro-level too.
The public nature of my job has given me a rich resource of persons including heads of government departments, CEOs, across fields whom I networked for writing my news and feature articles.

* As chief of news bureau, I am involved in day-to day management /administration of news flow (24 hours), work allocation for reporters/photographers, managing photography and graphic elements for all news/feature stories from my bureau, preparing the day's news list as member of the news management committee in TOI and responsible for news/features content in the city section of the newspaper.
All news/feature reports need to have my clearance before they go for publication.

MY JOURNALISTIC SKILLS

* I started off as a trainee journalist soon after completing my graduation in Journalism. As a reporter, I covered all beats -- ranging from education, health, rural development, science and technology, women and child welfare, industries, and government.

* I have written more than 2,000 news articles, features, interviews and special investigation reports on these subjects. My specialization was writing all aspects of education - from primary to post-graduate education, covering all premier institutes and foreign universities too. I headed the education team for TOI and authored over 200 weekly columns on campus buzz.

* Many of my news reports have resulted in policy decisions, impacted individuals, and society at large. I have many breaking stories to my credit. I was the youngest journalist in the newspaper to be given an exclusive column.

* I have authored many special reports on malnutrition, urban infrastructure, midday meal, child labor, health, and education.

* I have attended many international conferences on health, technology, urban issues and education as India correspondent for TOI.

SCHOLARSHIPS/AWARDS AND CITATIONS
=======================================

* I am a recipient of the International Visitors Leadership Programme (IVLP) -- the premier professional exchange programme of the United States (US) government in 2010.

* Recipient of the European Union scholarship for a malnutrition project.

* Won the best young journalist award of the Zee group for my outstanding writing on education.

* Won the Namma Bengaluru best journalist award (through citizens nominations) for outstanding contribution to the betterment of Bengaluru in 2013.

EDUCATIONAL QUALIFICATIONS:
Majors in Journalism, English Literature and Psychology

PERSONAL INFORMATION/

email: sseethalakshmi2006@gmail.com

ends

9

HOW TO COMPETE IN ANY NICHE AND WIN!
- DOUGLAS KONG, REGIONAL DIRECTOR AT THE ALPHA GROUP SINGAPORE

What do you do when you suddenly lost your job and income and your career overnight disappeared? To some people this was so bad that they lost all hope and plunged into a depression so severe, that suicide may be viewed as the answer to problems. Yes, it can be that devastating.

That happened to me when I was found guilty of professional misconduct. I was indeed upset for a little while, but after that, I figured that nothing was to be gained by remaining in that state of brooding and negativism and after some deliberation, I decided to move on in life. With my skills in stress management, psychoanalysis, and group dynamics and having worked with CEO's and C-suite executives since the early 1990's, I decided to take a turn in my career and started to train as an Executive Coach and management consultant. It was not easy but over time, I established myself firmly in my current niche and role.

Life had not been a breeze for me at all. Throughout my childhood because of my physical weakness, I was occasionally bullied. I compensated by excelling in studies. Because of changing government regulations, I missed getting a scholarship and prior to entering university, I suffered from a depression. Then in my final year in med school, I failed 1 subject in the finals, and again I was in depression a second time. From these experience, I realized how painful depression can be, and I took up psychiatry to understand myself and to help others. That's how I ended up specializing in stress management.

It was because of stress management that I was roped in by my friends in the industry to conduct stress management workshops with companies such as Singapore Airlines, Port of Singapore Authority and IBM to name a few. And again because of that, I found myself working with CEOs and C-suite executives initially with stress and then got consulted with their organizational problems. I found that many organizational issues often revolved around relationship conflicts and I could use my knowledge of psychoanalysis to bear on it. I also developed an interest in-group dynamics as a result.

I was depressed a third time when my godfather had a heart attack as a result of business failure. I was badly affected as I was quite close to him. He was like a mentor to me. By then I had turned to self-help books to help me cope with the stresses of life. Through self-help books, I learned techniques to help myself cope better and learned how to strengthen myself against succumbing to pressures and demands that normally cripple you. One notable lesson I learned from all these was that there are answers to almost anything. But you need patience, and diligence to look for them so that you will pull yourself through. I later learned that a positive outlook and a cheerful disposition helped very much(my wife, an extrovert was great in transforming me here) to make me more resilient and being able to bounce back from stress.

I was then a lecturer in the University but found my job stressful because of office politics and intense professional rivalry.

With another colleague, I resigned, set up a practice and started to run stress management courses and helping quite a number of business organizations with their problems. I had a thriving clinical practice and a subsidiary company engaged in management consultancy helping companies as detailed above. Over time, I became known as a Key Opinion Leader in my industry and a leading speaker at many conferences in Asia and ASEAN countries. I was frequently sponsored by the Pharma industry for frequent trips overseas, and I believed it was this that caused professional jealousy about me leading to attempts to cut me down.

That's how I feel, and so, when the problems of 5 years ago surfaced, I followed the advice that I have often given to people and executives facing tough situations. It was very difficult to follow my own advice, which was easy to dispense but hard to implement. But I persevered. As I redefined my career and role in life, I had to relearn a lot of stuff and acquiring new skill sets. I just did it. I managed to maintain my sanity by falling back on my relationships; my wife of 40 years whom I knew as a childhood sweetheart. My school friends from both my secondary and high school were extremely supportive. They supported me by believing in me and encouraged me to do what my heart told me to do.

Besides relationships, it was my hobbies that allowed me an outlet. Music, I enjoy both classical and popular, as well as golf. Both these hobbies gave me immense pleasure, countering the negativity in my life and helped me to restore my psychological balance. They made me forget all the negative and tough memories I had. More importantly, these hobbies helped to connect me to a larger group of people and they gave me much pleasure that was the best antidote to all the problems I was then facing.

With all these support, I came through and established myself as an Executive Coach and Management Consultant. I studied intensely about business growth, how businesses thrive, why they failed, and how businesses can grow and scale up in size and complexity. I found it intriguing that many businesses failed because of lack of resources. I found it surprising that whether they succeed or fail, many business owners have no clue as to what happened and why they succeed or fail. I deepened my knowledge in strategic management and went deep into strategic processes of strategy formulation and implementation. This last item is most important. Of those who had a meaningful strategy, more than two thirds implement their strategy badly. Slowly, a coherent picture emerged.

I have now successfully evolved a framework with which to help businesses. Based on sound empirical principles and strong theoretical foundation, this framework was robust enough for application to both large and small companies. The basis of this framework is a robust and altruistic mindset that attracts customers. The structure of this framework is built on your skill set and your response to the competitive environment because of your strengths and value system. Coupled with reasonable goals, this is transformed into a strategy to survive and to thrive in the market place. Now you need determination and focus to implement your strategy with determination, courage, and focus. It was most relevant to small companies for that is where the failure rates are the highest. I have now found the mission of my life!

So, are you struggling in your business? Confused, frustrated and tired out by everything you have tried and perplexed as to what to do next? Have you found a way out of your difficulties before you drown in your own problems? Fear not, many have gone before you, including me. I have been there myself and saw what was it like, what needed to be done.

You would need a mentor or a coach, for that was what I seek at the lowest points of my life. I engaged the services of up to 3 different coaches. Coaching helped me to discover my strengths and steered me to the choice most suitable for me. Coaching helped me to discover my inner strength to focus on what matters and to persist in my mission, no matter what. Coaching and coaches help simply because we are our own worst enemy. More important, we need to be disciplined and focused on working in the right direction. Coaches serve as accountability partners in this regard. An accountability partner is one who will call you out when you start to slip, procrastinate and get sidetrack by every shining object that comes your way. Because of coaches who were my accountability partners keeping me on track, I was able to achieve again once more.

Because of what I have been through in the last 5 years, I can understand the struggles, heartaches, and difficulties faced by startup entrepreneurs and business owners. I know the passion, the pain and the pleasure that comes from each tiny success along the way. It is a tough journey, a lonely journey where most people do not quite understand you. It's a journey that is built on hope in the future which only you can see and only your strongest supporters will believe with you. I know, for I have been there myself. I believe you too can do it, but you must know that the forces that will keep you from success are strong. We know that 96% of small businesses fail within 10 years, and we know that of those still around, many are struggling to keep afloat. You need more than passion to sustain you.

You need help. Just like me, I seek for coaches to learn from them and get professional support. I strongly recommend you do the same so that you can ensure your own success. Having gone on before, I can offer myself and my team of experts to you for your learning and be used as your support. Let me walk with you to your success that is just before you. Allow me to be your guide to conquer the difficulties and challenges of your life, as I have done so in life. Let this be your turn to win.

To contact the writer, write: douglas@optimalzoneperformance.com

Douglas Kong

Douglas Kong is the Regional Director at The Alpha Group Singapore.

His professional goal is to help entrepreneurs and small businesses to function optimally and achieve the goals they have set for themselves. That's what Douglas does as an Executive and Business Coach, especially in the context of The Alpha Group, the premier peer-to-peer external Board of Reference and Mastermind groups for small businesses.

Douglas was previously a psychiatrist where, besides prescribing medication, he has consistently helped patients to resolve underlying issues whether they be personality problems, social and communication problems, family or work stress issues using various psychological techniques such as psychoanalytic techniques, cognitive behavioral skills, hypnosis, EMDR and group therapy.

Douglas has also worked with organizations providing stress management workshops, OD intervention, group facilitation and other interventions.

Currently, he is using all these clinical skills, aided by a newly acquired coaching skillset to help CEO's and Senior Executives to function at a higher level, and resolve conflicts common to organizations, interpersonal relationships and personal inadequacies and shortcomings in The Alpha Group setting, as a Performance and Leadership Coach and GOLD Coach. Douglas is practice-oriented and focuses on real people and real problems, working out a solution that best fits with the circumstances.

10

DON'T SETTLE FOR 7, GO FOR 10!
- SHANE RAM, EXECUTIVE COACH TO CEOS, SENIOR LEADERS AND ENTREPRENEURS, GLOBAL KEYNOTE SPEAKER, PROPERTY INVESTOR AND AUTHOR

Are you successful but feel like there is more to life and business than what you are doing right now?

Have you ever asked yourself, 'is this it, is this what I will be doing for the next 20 years?

Do you feel like you are not fulfilled?

Do you see other people doing what you would really like to be doing? People who are less qualified than you, people who started out with less money than you, people who are younger than you?

Now imagine a life where you are doing what you love, living on purpose and creating an impact on the world and there is no difference between work and play. IMAGINE having multiple streams of income, time freedom so you can do what you want, with whom you want and when you want and leave a legacy.

You don't need to imagine anymore, there are people out there living this life and I am here to share with you a proven process to get you there.

I had progressed quickly in my early career and became a C-Suite Executive at the age of 31. I was having success in my career and earning a good 6-figure income, had a company paid up Mercedes Benz, a couple nice vacations for the year, what I call the 7 life. But I knew something was missing. I knew there was more to life than what I was doing and that I was meant to create a bigger impact in the world, leave a great legacy and simply function at a higher level of consciousness and being, what I call the 10 Life. I did not know who to speak with and what were the steps I needed to take so I started reading and learning and then developed my own principles, which I now share with people all over the world with my various programs.

I had my spark of what I really wanted to do and how best to create impact in the world when I was 27 years old while looking at a personal development program on TV but I did not know what to do and who to speak with to bring my idea to life. That spark remained dormant for 10 years and it was painful because I was not living what I was meant to be doing, I was not living my fullest potential, I was not fulfilled and I knew there was more for me to do in this world. As a coach and a mentor, I am now being too many people what I needed when I was 27 so that people do not have to go through the agony for a whole 10 years and some people a lifetime of unfulfillment.

A great majority of the world is generally dissatisfied and one of the reasons is that people are not doing the thing they were meant to do. I believe that the lack of fulfillment comes from living a life that is not in alignment with our purpose or a purpose. You are placed here on this earth with a purpose, with a song to sing and unless you find that purpose you will never be as happy and fulfilled. Because of this missing piece (purpose), most people try to fill it with things. Things like cars, hobbies, shopping, a mistress and even business, which only makes them temporarily happy. The purpose is at is the core of my program called Scientific Happiness, which is a proven system based on science to help people find the career and personal fulfillment. The programs help people find happiness and fulfillment through purpose in all areas of life including business, health, emotions, relationships, parenting, career, and finances. When you begin to live on purpose, resources, people and circumstance come into your life and success begins to chase you. I have written about this in my book 'How To Get Success To Start Chasing You, Instead of You Chasing Success'

Think of something you want to achieve in your life. Ask yourself why you want to achieve this. When you come up with an answer, again ask yourself why do you want to achieve this (the first answer) and what would it do for you. Keep going and repeat the same questions to every answer you come up with. Most likely your final answer will be some sort of feeling, a feeling of fulfillment, a feeling of satisfaction, a feeling that you are valued, a feeling of accomplishment etc. The reason why you do anything is ultimate to achieve a feeling and the most important of that is Happiness. Aristotle said that 'Happiness is the meaning and purpose of life, the whole aim, and end of human existence'

Scientific Happiness has really transformed many people's lives and one of my great success stories is Joannah. After completing the Scientific Happiness program she gave a testimonial when I came across Shane's program, I was in a very dark place in my life; confused, depressed, heartbroken, despondent and cynical are some of the words I can use to describe how I felt. I believe I was working very hard to overcome these emotions, however, dealing with them on my own proved difficult and it was easy to slip back into old habits. Shane helped me to truly face my fears and "demons" and somehow, somewhere, deep down inside me I was able to find the determination and purpose that was missing from my life for so long.

For the first time in my adult life, I can truly say that I am happy and I am happy not because someone else made me happy but I am happy because I am finally comfortable in my own skin and living a purpose-driven life filled with passion and positivity.' After completing the program Joannah left her job in procurement and went on to open a great New York Style Gourmet Vegan Restaurant.

From a small village in Trinidad in the Caribbean, my childhood was marked by poverty, domestic violence, and family illiteracy. I did not have electricity or running water until I was 10, almost dying of starvation when I was 5 and had to study for my 11+ exam with a kerosene lamp. With my beloved scout leader passing at an early age, I had no real mentor or guide to pull him through a tough early childhood, so I had to develop my own principles of success and went on to defy the odds by completing two masters' degrees, one in Strategic Thinking and one in business. I always worked hard despite my situation and did well in academics and sport but never got the recognition from my father. The unconscious desire to be recognized by my father served as the driving force behind my competitive nature and achievement orientation. I later realized that this should not be the driver of what I do, this was not the way.

Despite me trying to be recognized by my father as my driving force, there were other concepts and principles that really propelled my transformation. One principle that really worked well for me and I believe it will work well for you is to approach life with openness and adventure. My openness allowed me to learn so many things and have so many different life experiences. Ironically, my parents were really responsible for this because they always allowed me to try new things. With openness, you get to discover what you really care about and believe and what you don't but when you are not open you run the big risk of missing so many opportunities and realizations.

This openness and adventure facilitated another key success principle for me, which is to be a constant seeker and learner. As a real child I was always inquisitive and wanted to know stuff and this has stayed with me up to today. I spend an insane amount of time and money on reading and learning.

There are four levels of learning with increasing levels of effectiveness and they are:
1) Formal training and education.
2) Learning by Doing.
3) Learning from a Coach or Mentor.
4) Learning by teaching.

The most profound learning experiences for me have come from my coaches and mentors. I have found that the fastest way to learn is to find someone who has accomplished what you want to accomplish or has helped other people to accomplish the same thing and follow them.

Being a workshop facilitator has also helped me tremendously as I always had to be reading to keep up with the current research, tools, and techniques in the various fields that I train. This really increased my value and this allowed me to deliver more value to my customers. I became a walking, talking, the value-breeding machine, which made me one of the most valuable people in my industry. I now wow my audiences with little known but interesting, informative and practical presentations.

Coming to the realization that I have absolutely nothing to lose in life, that I came to this earth with nothing and will leave with nothing was the main idea that gave me the final push to leave my job and start my various businesses. When you have an idea and you are scared because of the potential risks involved, remember that you really have nothing to lose. The moment you realize that you have nothing to lose, you have everything to gain.

These three principles of Openness and Adventure, Constant seeker and Leaner and Nothing to Lose, plus the seven others in the program Don't Settle for 7, Go for 10! when applied, will significantly advance your life and your business. These are what propelled me from poor, no electricity, no running water, with parents who never finished school to having 2 Masters Degrees, becoming a C-Suite Executive at 31 with a 6 figure income and able to travel all over the world.

I had the life, what I now call the 7 life, that a lot of people would be very happy with but I knew there was more. In the downturn of 2009 the company I worked for had cut back on their HR projects and there was little to do and I had more free time. So I had a 6-figure income, fully paid up Mercedes Benz and free time, perfect! I used my free time sometimes to play golf and walking down the first fairway one morning I said to myself, Shane this is not it, you are meant to do more in this world, and you are meant to create more impact.

This is when I decided to pursue the 10 Life, a life where I create more IMPACT with more people, a life where I can create and leave a LEGACY for generations and a life where I can live at a HIGHER LEVEL OF CONSCIOUSNESS AND BEING.

Could anything be better? Waking up every day knowing that lots of people are smiling because you choose to impact lives, making the world a better place. Each person has the potential of making a positive impact on the world. It all depends on what you do with what you have. Success is not only to be measured by the amount of money you possess or the position you attain but rather in how you use both. Position and money could be squandered or abused, but they can be used to help others. When you love people and have the desire to make a profound, positive IMPACT, then you will have accomplished the meaning to truly live.

In the last decade or so you would have seen many ultra-successful people concentrating more on IMPACT. They would have reached the pinnacle in business and industry but they realized that that was actually not the pinnacle of life. They are now focusing on how they can impact the world. There is a great opportunity for you now to combine your profession with your impact so that you don't have to first have success and then create IMPACT. If your profession or business is centered on IMPACT you are on your way to a more fulfilling life, a 10 Life. Many times it's easier than you think because it is not about changing WHAT you do, but WHY you do it.

What is going to be your LEGACY? What are you going to start that is not going to end with your death? To live in the mind and hearts of the generations who will follow you is to cheat death and to really live a worthwhile life.

If you were asked, "What is your great grandfather's name?" Many of us would say, "I do not know". The reason is that they did not pass on a family legacy. The Rockefellers, Kennedys, Marriotts, and Hiltons are examples of how generational wealth is passed on. These multi-generational families have passed on several successful businesses known as dynasties. In the battle against multi-generational poverty, growing evidence has supported asset building as an increasingly important means to provide upward financial mobility and pathways to passing on wealth for a positive economic future. Legacy planning is an important component to creating a strong financial foundation, ensuring a future for the next generations and making certain that your wishes will be carried out after you're gone — whether the assets will be left to family, organizations or charities.

Most of the world is living in a hysterical blindness and deafness, a mindless pursuit of pleasure, celebration of ignorance and egomania. The world needs you as leaders and professionals to operate at a HIGHER LEVEL OF CONSCIOUSNESS AND BEING.

To me, A HIGHER LEVEL OF CONSCIOUSNESS is allowing inspiration, intuition, and guidance from a higher intelligence to flow in everything that I do in my business and family life. In this way, life is happening around me and that feeling is absolutely exhilarating and liberating.

A HIGHER LEVE OF BEING is about elevating and expanding your thinking from its current state of looking at the world through lenses and filters created by a concoction of ideas placed into you by others -by parents, teachers, and authority figures. This is achieved through developing critical thought, social intelligence and self-control.

Higher levels of consciousness involve non-ordinary organs of awareness such as higher intellect (Thought and Discernment), Higher Feeling (Sentience or Appreciation), Higher will, Higher Love, and Higher Apperception (Inspiration or Intuition). The beauty of moving to a HIGHER LEVEL OF BEING is that you are not 'becoming' anything – you are simply awakening to your true nature and awakening your dormant faculties.

It is about moving from thinking that your life is just a random series of events that happen because you did it right or you did it wrong. It is a sense of an intelligent unfolding that is revealing itself to you and through you.

Take a moment now to feel how different that is from the way you usually perceive Life: as something happening to you that needs to be controlled, fixed and changed. Imagine what it would be like to let go of the whole game of resisting Life and instead to trust it. In this trust, you could then open to it, listen to it, and grow from every encounter.

Did I just take you to another level?

You are born to create IMPACT in the world, you have the potential to create a LEGACY for your family and future generations and you can master life by living at a HIGHER LEVEL OF CONSCIOUSNESS.

Remember Don't Settle for 7, Go for 10! For mentorship and coaching to get you there, please visit www.shaneram.com or email iam@shaneram.com

Shane Ram

Shane Ram is the CEO of STEP HR Consulting, Founder of Scientific Happiness™, Property Investor, Founder of Don't Settle for 7™, executive coach, author and a sought-after global keynote speaker. Shane works with CEOs, corporations, 6-7 Figure business owners, and entrepreneurs to increase revenue grow their businesses and live more fulfilling lives.

At the tender age of 31, Shane became a C-Suite Executive and helped organizations with employees from 70 different countries to manage through disruptive change and rapid growth. As head of the corporate university, Shane trained senior leaders in human resource management, coaching, and leadership which resulted in managers becoming better CEOs, a giant leap in leadership capabilities which fostered company growth, launching six profitable new markets in 3 years.

Due to extensive experience in coaching and training senior leaders and CEOs, Shane set up STEP HR Consulting and quickly launched in 5 countries doing training in the areas of Leadership, Emotional Intelligence, Communication, Change Management, Coaching and Human Resource Management. These programs elevated the individual performance of company leaders and resulted in better work relationships and ultimately increased revenues amidst relentless change.

In 2013 Shane launched a business in sales and built a sales team of over 4,000 distributors in 17 countries doing over $2M in sales helping entrepreneurs launch their businesses.

Working with senior managers, CEOs, and entrepreneurs, Shane found that while many people, including himself, were successful, they weren't necessary fulfilled or happy. Shane founded Scientific Happiness, which is a proven system based on science to help people find both success and fulfillment in their lives in the areas of business, relationships, health, career, parenting, and finances. From Shane's years of experience training and coaching senior leaders and entrepreneurs, he found that most people are playing at a level way below their potential and are settling for less than they deserve, Shane created Don't Settle for 7, Go for 10! The program provides a much-needed blueprint for leaders and entrepreneurs to increase their wealth, and build global businesses, create confidence and reach their highest potential physically and financially.
Shane has traveled extensively training and speaking and is a regular at HR Conferences across the world and has shared the same stage with people like of Malcolm Gladwell. He has trained and consulted in the UK, Africa, North and Central America, South Pacific and most Caribbean countries. Shane has also worked across many industries including telecommunications, food and beverage, technology, government, utilities, financial services, hospitality, health, and manufacturing.
From a small village in Trinidad in the Caribbean, Shane's childhood was marked by poverty, domestic violence, and family illiteracy. He did not have electricity or running water until he was 10, almost dying of starvation when he was 5 and had to study for this 11+ exam with a kerosene lamp. With his beloved scout leader passing at an early age, Shane had no real mentor or guide to pull him through a tough early childhood, so he had to develop his own principles of success and went on to defy the odds by having two masters' degrees, one in Strategic Thinking and one in business.

Shane is a published author of How to Get Success to Start Chasing You.

Shane is a sought-after global keynote speaker and works with CEOs and corporate companies and entrepreneurs to grow their business. His strikingly effective coaching process shows individuals and corporate teams how to create the personal lives they want while becoming a megastar at work. To book a time to speak with Shane go to meet me.so/shaneram. To book Shane for events and seminars go to www.shaneram.com or www.stepadvisors.net, call 1-868-350-STEP or email at iam@shaneram.com

11

LISTEN! SOMETHING BIG IS CALLING!
- BY DIANA DENTINGER, INSPIRATIONAL SPEAKER & FOUNDER OF THE MEANING OF LIFE SCHOOL

We are so fine tuned to focus our attention on the outside world, to fit in, to follow in other people's footsteps and to fail, often just like them, at finding happiness. Instead, what I have found, is that when you turn your attention inside, you "hear" life altering suggestions that lead you down a more fulfilling life path; one that is waiting for you to explore, if you'd just be still and listen.

Do you know what happens if you only use thoughts, feelings, reasoning, will power and ethics to drive your actions? You stay within the boundaries of your beliefs and the limits of your past.

What is it that can open you up to limitlessness? Is there something else? In my over 25 years of training and coaching, when I talk about this "something else" often people shun it, deny it or are afraid to talk about it. Yet all great people of our past and present admit the value of what they call "intuition" or higher intelligence.

Many people ask me how I "ended up" in Europe so this is the story I wish to share with you about being guided by my intuition.

In the summer of 1984, I was walking down the street near Westminster Abbey in London with college friends. We had just spent three months traveling all over Europe after graduation from our US Universities and this city was our final destination before returning home.

"I know I have to stay, but how?" I asked myself. I had fallen in love with the beauty of Florence, the excitement of Rome and the romance of Venice. These places moved my soul profoundly. I felt like I had walked their streets before. Even when I was in Germany, there was a feeling of comfort. It was so hard to explain, but one thing was for sure, I had to find a way to live in Europe.

The next day I would be on a plane back home and my heart sunk. A "voice" told me not to go. "Diana, you belong in Europe", it said.

So I mustered up the courage to call my dad at work and with a pocket full of coins, I stepped into one of the red phone booths on the corner adjacent to Big Ben. I still know exactly where it is. His secretary answered and she said he was in an important meeting. I responded with: "This is very important too". After a few minutes and quite a few shillings, he got on the line.

At first I thought I would ask him what he thought about me staying, but my money was running out and I only had time to say, "Dad, I am not going to be on the plane tomorrow. I am going to Germany. I want to find a job and study German."

He did not take it well. He spurt out a hundred objections in only sixty seconds and when I heard the signal that the call was finishing, I said, "I will call you when I get to Germany." And the line went dead. I felt relieved. I felt confident. This was the best thing for me.

The next morning, I left my backpack and belongings at Victoria train station on purpose, and accompanied my friends to the airport to say goodbye. I tried to get reimbursed for my ticket without any luck. Now it looked like I was not only staying in Europe, but even stuck.

I took the noon train that headed south, crossed the English Channel and arrived in Munich the next morning. What I remember most about that journey was that I felt so true to myself. I did not feel afraid. I did not feel alone. I did not feel worried. I felt pure connection.

What happened over the next month was quite amazing. Upon arrival in Munich, I went to the American Consulate to find out how I could get a job. They suggested I become an au pair. One woman there was so helpful and set up an interview a day for the entire next week. There were many families looking for English speaking babysitters.

But things did not go the way I imagined. None of those families really felt right. I started to get discouraged. I wondered if I really should have stayed. I questioned if my intense desire to be in Europe was right. My money was running out so I needed to get a plan B. I thought I would give it a few more days and then go find a waitressing job, maybe in the south of France.

The next day though, I got a call from the women at the Consulate. She got in touch with me through the youth hostel phone number where I was staying. She said she thought she had the perfect family for me. Sure enough it was and I started work the same day!

They had an adorable British au pair who was returning home in another four days. She showed me what chores I needed to do for the family, and in those evenings she took me out to meet people. There was quite a fun group of international people in the Au Pair Association she belonged to. It was similar to a modern Meet Up or Internations group with both young men and women.

Through one of my new girlfriends there, in just a few weeks, I met the man who would become my husband. He was Italian. I had seen myself in "my dream life" living in Italy. Somehow Munich "called" me as a first stepping-stone to get where I really belonged.

Many times in our lives we get that "calling" or "flash" inviting us to do something. In that split second it is a real voice, fast yet calm, intense yet patient. It is void of fear. It is genuine. It indicates the way.

Then our mind, our ego or our rationality step in to run the show. We start to hear another "voice". But this one is of doubt and duality. We get wrapped up in a dynamic of flight or fight, pleasure or pain, right or wrong. The voice cautions us not to make mistakes.

Have you lived either of these situations before? Have you ever thought you "heard a voice"? Did you follow its suggestions?

Many of my clients, and especially top entrepreneurial men, have confided in me that their intuition is what helps them make the best business decisions. And then they add: "But this is something I don't dare say to the Board!" Why is it then that this "all inspiring" quality, for those who use it, is kept such a secret?

The "voice" has come on loud and clear many a times in my life and indicated people to meet and places to go. I have found job opportunities and even created my own training methodologies thanks to this guidance.

One of the most profound and transformational experiences with the "voice" came in the year 2004 when I was in the Paris airport on a connecting flight to Cincinnati. I was looking around at the duty free perfumes when I was "told" to go to the restroom. Without thinking, I walked to the ladies room.

There was one woman in line. She had dreadlocks and an incredibly beautiful amethyst stone necklace. I reached over to touch it and she said, "I'm sorry, I don't let anyone touch it. It's a healing stone." I had "asked" to meet a healer in my intentions just the week before since one of my favorite cousins, my age, had been diagnosed with cancer.

Sure enough she and I were on the same plane and even in the same row. And sure enough she lived in the same city as my cousin. She said she was "called" to be on that plane and left Saint Petersburg Russia a week earlier than planned. This woman was a catalyst for many things in my life, taking me to Brazil and New Zealand to study energy and meditation practices.

Had I not listened to that rapid-fire message while at the duty free shop, I do not know what my life would look like now. I guess I never will. What I do know is that the times I listened, things always worked out well.

As a Corporate Consultant, I am open-minded and

openhearted. My clients find me very practical, and they also feel that there is something more to my coaching than what meets the eye. It has been challenging for me to break free of what they could think about the "something else" and it has been an empowering process to learn to stand solid in my gifts.

I have learned to trust that spontaneous "transmission" of information. It's not calculated, elaborated or confabulated. It just is. And it comes unexpectedly, at the right time, in the right place for the right person.

Years ago I let diplomacy and "I shouldn't be so straightforward" get in the way of sharing my perceptions with clients (and family members). Then the more I became comfortable speaking from this perspective, the more other people opened up that they too had these experiences.

I love my intuitive nature. I am sure I was born with it, just like everyone else, and I am happy I have also refined it. Over the years, the "voice" has spoken to me many times.

Sometimes it comes as a buddy who nudges me to do something. Other times as a soft caress. It told me "important children will be born" the minute before I walked down the aisle to get married. It was so moving my eyes swelled with tears. Then the music "here comes the bride music" started and I glanced over at my dad. I surely couldn't share what had just transpired. He probably thought I was choked up for the ceremony.

This "message" has been a guiding principle in parenting my four children. In their hearts and in their minds, I am sure each and every one of them feel they are here for a higher purpose. I have not spoiled them with lots of objects and things, but I have let them know that they are important in my dialogue with them. When I go back to visit my hundreds of relatives in USA, they all comment on how good my kids are. It humbles me to know I have done well.

The "voice" has helped me overcome obstacles in many times of trouble. Living far from home and raising my 4 children pretty much on my own, it has been a source of support. For as much as heartwarming Skype calls with my father and mother have shortened the distance, having "someone" or "something else" close by to count on has been a relief.

It has helped me stay positive and keep the faith. Even when it warned me of accidents, I was prepared for the news, the hospital stays and the loss. I feel fortunate because the "voice" teaches me to worry less and trust more.

Most of all, it guides me to live my life's purpose in ever bigger and better ways. It nourishes my self-confidence and gives me clear signs to confirm that I am on the right path.

By sharing these simple stories from my life, I wish to encourage you to turn your attention inside. Be still. And in the silence of your inner world, listen if there is a voice calling you to something bigger too.

Diana Dentinger

Diana Dentinger is an Innovative Change Maker and Influential Thought Leader who inspires you to Play All Out in Life. In her Number One Self Help Transformation book "Modus Vivendi - Your Life Your Way" she takes you on a journey to discover your core personality, purpose and unexplored potential.

STARDOM BOOKS

12

HOW CONSULTATIVE FINESSE BEATS TYPICAL FIGHT VS. FLIGHT IN STRESSFUL WORK SITUATIONS

- BY ROLF FOSTER-JORGENSEN, GLOBAL CONSULTING AUTHORITY, CERTIFIED HIGH PERFORMANCE COACH, AWARD-EARNING FACILITATOR/TRAINER

Think back to a time when you felt embarrassed at work. Perhaps a boss disciplined or someone else ridiculed your work, or you just said something on a group call that you wished could have been retracted and erased from everyone's memory. I'm not trying to make you feel discouraged, as everyone has had similarly unpleasant experiences. It's difficult to deny that it was stressful and hurt, even if you rationalize that the conflict made you stronger. Truthfully, those are instances where our inner drive kicks in to want to either fight or flee.

My older brother passed away a few years ago and, though I loved him dearly, there was no denying that he struggled all his life to hold a steady job. The main reason was because he was brilliant, at least as measured by IQ tests. Now you may say how can a brilliant person really struggle when that should open many doors? The problem was that something always happened that exposed his feeling smarter than his boss, and he failed to learn how NOT to say so. Anyone could easily get fired after telling a boss that he or she is stupid, right? Classic "fight" scenario, eh?

I know. You say that you've learned greater self-discipline to not get fired that way. Even if you said something that was perceived to be rude, yet not bad enough to get fired, there was likely some immediate verbal or nonverbal feedback about inappropriate behavior. However, think back to times when you may NOT have said anything, even when you knew you were right, particularly if others acted forcefully in those situations. Choosing NOT to speak up about your insights and opinions is a form of "fleeing". For those working in a friendly, supportive environment, it may not seem to be an issue, yet trying to measure the intangible career impact of "fleeing" inaction can be difficult unless there were a way to bring it to your attention.

Do you ever wish you had some tools to better understand what, why and how others are likely to act BEFORE a situation escalates to a fight vs. flight decision? That is where the online and face-to-face Consultative Skills methods I've designed and developed over 30+ years provide a safer, middle ground. It's the FINESSE sitting between Fight vs. Flight options, that you can subtly apply without fanfare or disruption that may feel uncharacteristic to how you prefer to work.

In fact, that is how I work best, quietly behind the scenes, helping others look good in a respectful, discrete, confidential manner. Before you judge that as not your style, please understand it was not always mine either. I'm living proof that anyone can learn to be a subtle influencer.

For background, I'm an unassuming Canadian who grew up in the US in a functional family of two parents and two siblings. My

Father was a Lutheran pastor and Mother a part-time bookkeeper, happily married since age 25. While that may sound boring, it certainly did not seem so to me. My Dad loved variety, a trait I thankfully learned to embrace and instill in our children. About every 2-6 years, my Dad would accept a different "call" (how you moved in the church). They varied from inner city to suburban, rural to international, start-up congregations to established multilingual institutions. He was the first US exchange pastor in Oslo because he spoke fluent Norwegian. Upon arrival, he was surprised when told that sermons were expected to be 3+ hours long. I was only 8, so I thought EVERY Dad did public speaking as their job. That helped me naturally develop the confidence to act, sing, play timpani/ percussion, and serve others as a professional consultant/ trainer/ facilitator.

I earned a Bachelor of Arts four-year Liberal Arts degree in Political Science with Urban Studies Concentration (minor) from a prestigious and rigorous school. Yet that included changing my major five times before settling on what was more popular at the time than my real passion for business. The PolySci degree included internships at government bureaucracies and with national political leaders during particularly scandalous times (when isn't there, eh?). Disillusioned, I accepted a job with a global not-for-profit business education organization, youthfully rationalizing that I would at least be idealistically "helping people". I quickly realized that political science knowledge applied wherever there were groups forming to influence others. I was honoured that others identified me for fast-track training, catapulting over more seasoned staff to become the organization's youngest staff president (the title used in only the top 25 markets). In that role, I hired excellent staff, recruited and served a high-level board of directors of Fortune 500 C-Suite executives, and authored the then largest national grant from a major foundation. I learned a lot about executives, including that they put their pants on the same as anyone else and you just need to proactively anticipate their needs while wisely using their time and influence. Some of them helped me start my consulting practice when only age 30. Still, I wish someone had shown that immature me some quick and effective tools such as I've recently developed. My economical SituationalALERTness^{SM} online video training available 24/7 helps to anticipate how and why subgroups are likely to act BEFORE you might need their support or lack of resistance. My CHALLENGE execYOUtives℠ online program guides you through various levels of consultative wording for respectfully and safely challenging a boss, or anyone in authority, in ways that enhance your career.

I've often been asked how can I be a "consultant" without grey hair or a Ph.D.? Yes, I've subcontracted many with those credentials onto my teams when a client seemed initially nervous. Yet that usually only initially propped open a door. They understandably also ask, "What are you doing to help me today?" Quite frankly, I've proven that practical real life experience that unselfishly fosters insight and wisdom also earns trust and respect…and repeat business.

Did I test my limits along the journey? Definitely. My wife and I have started, acquired and sold numerous businesses, including multi-million dollar ones with up to 150 employees. She proved to have greater patience than I when dealing with some of our managers who did not see things that needed to be done with their direct reports, even after being told what to do. I finally realized that my trying to "tell" them what to do was the root cause of their not following through once I left the premises to visit our other locations. Why would they internalize and implement MY processes when my only consistency was to criticize and press for faster results?

Ironically, that was not the way I was simultaneously treating my consulting clients in the early years of our mainstay business. No, I consultatively coached, good humouredly challenged, and gently guided them toward committing to their own priorities. In fact, that was so successful that it led me to a major epiphany. Why not treat EVERYONE that way and no longer feel stressed about others seemingly letting ME down. Plus, consistently applying consultative behaviors with everyone meant not having to remember what was said to whom as nothing harmful would come back to bite me later.

Do Yourself a F.A.V.O.U.R.

Now, whenever I feel any negativity toward anything, I apply a simple process I call, "Do Yourself a F.A.V.O.U.R." (Yes, it's Canadian spelling). It stands for:

F = Feel   Embrace your feelings, regardless of business style or situation

A = Acknowledge   Catch yourself as early as possible when thinking negatively

V = Value   Value every relationship more than any atypical incident or thought

O = Own It   Don't blame anyone else for your own reactions to any situation

U = Understand   Remember you're dealing with behaviors, not the whole person

R = Release   Give yourself permission to let it go, forgive yourself, and just move on

Thinking back, those struggling managers helped me learn an important life lesson.

"Deal with people wherever they are at the moment, and help them stretch at their own pace to whatever changes they are willing to consider."

That helped me create a safe enough space for many clients to proactively grow into true high performers. (I later became one of the founding 100 members of global High Performance Coaches, as certified by the High Performance Academy).

Most of my clients for decades have been Fortune 500 executives, managers and support roles. That has meant signing confidentiality, non-disclosure and non-compete agreements. It has also meant no internal video, pictures or written testimonials (per legal department advice about ANY outside resource) despite extensive praise and repeat business. That is often part of the trade-off when earning access to such confidential areas as intellectual property/ trade secrets, competitive/ business intelligence, strategic planning meetings, etc. When other consultants ask me how to get started, I sometimes joke, "Be careful what you wish for unless you're willing to also accept their rules." So why am I now sharing my insights here and via my consultativeskills.com website? I've learned how to teach skills to others without violating the confidence of my short and long term clients.

Act Authentically Without Airs

A colleague once introduced me to a group as "…the wisest person I know." I quickly asked if he spelled that "wisest" or "wise-assed"? They laughed and he responded, "Now that you mention it – both". It was a reminder not to take myself too seriously or let ego get in the way of serving others.

My professional gratification comes from seeing how others apply learning gained from my training, coaching and facilitating. Let's explore a few actual examples. One was somewhat simple and the other more complex. Watch for subtle examples of what I call "consultative finesse".

A coaching client once commented that she admired how her boss would be in a group meeting of direct reports and peers, and just intently listen to a discussion. Then he would add some profoundly deeper perspective that would take the group outside the narrow company point of view. Finally, he would pose the most insightfully crafted questions that would stop people in their tracks while they thought about their answers.

After teaching her how to craft consultative questions, I asked her how she thought her boss might respond if she chose to just be candid and express her desire to emulate those learned traits. Perhaps ask him what ezines and periodicals he regularly reads that might help her professionally grow and offer greater value to the team. On our next call, she excitedly reported that he responded by offering her a leadership role on an exciting new project and set up a formal mentoring process together.

It's always refreshing to see the business rewards that can result from a little simple initiative about being more open to self-improvement and learning.

In another case, I was brought in as an independent subject matter expert by the Learning Organization (LO) division of a major company to meet with who they claimed to be a "domineering and stubborn" Sr. VP. Before agreeing to the meeting, I learned that apparently they were having difficulty convincing the executive to invest in their proposed "solution" to a problem he had approached them to fix. Based on my years of successfully conducting "consultative skills" classes within the firm, their solution included just uplifting my proven services. So I was supposedly to be at the meeting to soften up the prospect toward their "off-the-shelf" approach, even though the methods I teach are to customize solutions to best meet the client's needs. In other words, the learning team just wanted to get rid of the request by conveniently outsourcing their solution to a proven "vendor" with the assumption that my classes would suffice. When I asked what "needs requirements" steps they had previously taken to understand the request before proposing this particular solution, I was told that they had seen the same situation so many times that they didn't "waste this important executive's time" by typically exploring internal client issues. I hope you see the root cause of their dilemma.

At the meeting, I quickly confirmed this prospective client's dominant style and knew he would have greater respect if I showed that I could take charge of the meeting and steer it toward meeting HIS needs, not necessarily the learning division's representatives. By consultatively asking some open-ended questions, we quickly identified the challenges being faced by the executive, how they were impacting accomplishing his business goals, and some preferred behavioral outcomes that might address the gaps. I thought about how obvious it was to me that by simply tweaking some of the scenarios, or even the rigorous case study I use in my class, we could accomplish dramatic improvements. However, I shocked the learning reps by saying to the client that, depending on how quickly he wanted sustainable results, there were multiple methods of accomplishing the altered behaviors that would likely achieve his business goals. These could include training, coaching, mentoring, etc. each with their own trade-offs to consider. Even though the LO's solution would help me as the fulfillment contractor, I did this because I knew his dominant style preferred multiple options and risks/rewards factors from which to choose.

One of the LO reps immediately jumped in, thinking he would help his team and me, by pointing out that I had the highest satisfaction rankings of any of their external AND internal trainers and the client "should" select my maximum 30-person 3-day Consultative Skills classes. Appearing to feel boxed in, the client stated that he thought the best approach was to have his assistant (who was also in the conference room with us) travel to the six geographies of his division and conduct single meetings of about 150 people so as to minimize their time "away from productive work". It was that conflict that had prompted the LO setting up this particular meeting involving me, hoping that I would simply endorse their idea of repeatedly using my services.

I saw the situation differently and chose to apply another consultative approach (for which the client later complimented me for role modeling what he really wanted his team to learn to do with external customers). After honoring the talents and good intentions of the assistant, I asked them both what might happen if a sizeable percentage of his team either did not fully understand their message, or chose not to implement it. After the client's initial reaction about people risking their careers by ignoring his mandates, I could see him pondering the question more deeply. I then switched the emphasis to a question about the potential impact to HIM if those less-than-committed team members undermined achieving his division quarterly or annual goals. When the client acknowledged how bad that would be, I asked his assistant whether he believed "compliance" was the same as "buy-in" on their extended team. They both said no, and that opened the door to explore alternatives.

Again, rather than only pitch the LO solution of using my classes, I instead stated one way to possibly increase buy-in, even with groups of 150+ people at a time, could be to use expert "facilitation" skills in order to guide, rather than force, people to voluntarily buy in. I asked the assistant what training, if any, he had experienced in learning and practicing expert facilitation skills. He said he had none, after which a different LO rep boldly stated that to be one of Rolf's strongest skills. While I appreciated the compliment, her timing was off. It seemed too risky to appear to be pitting my strengths as an outside expert whom the client had just met, against his already trusted assistant. I instead moved to a more face-saving approach for the assistant.

I intentionally asked a rare closed question of whether they believed people learned more and retained the learning better when they had the opportunity to personally interact with peers and promptly apply the learning to their jobs. Everyone agreed that was most desirable, provided it also met budget, time and other typical constraints. I then asked a "what if" question to help broaden perspectives about different alternatives. I asked, "What if I were to team up with the assistant, providing my consultative skills and facilitation expertise as an available supplement to the assistant's lead and knowledge of the audience and the client's priorities?" The signs of relief on the assistant's face were noticeable to all, yet I didn't stop there with the obvious compromise because I still knew the trade-offs of trying to train groups of 150+ people were unlikely to meet the desired business goals. I asked if everyone would prefer not allowing individual team members to "hide" amongst a large group and possibly ignore the message without anyone realizing it until after some quarterly goals were not met. They all agreed that was undesirable.

Their OWN REPLIES presented the opening to discuss some benefits of training in smaller conspicuous groups. While I acknowledged in a neutral way that I could use my instructional design experience to develop some educational activities for any size groupings, including 150+, I also walked them through some examples where greater levels of interaction, team-building and reinforced learning seemed to work better within smaller groups with a common vision, mission, and directly perceived benefits.

Then a few important things happened, primarily because they all seemed more comfortable by that time. The assistant asked his boss if it was OK for me (Rolf) to conduct all the training and he would supplement it, as a background resource should any technical questions arise about the company. I offered to customize some of the training exercises to use real-life situations that their team would recognize and appreciate. The client agreed to all that and also committed to trying the smaller classes at one of their sites as a test. By providing the assistant with a graceful way to choose to bow out of the training leadership role, it allowed me to then ask the client to prepare a 1-2 minute video embarking his vision and priorities that could be played during each class delivery.

As expected, that test went so well that the client committed to my conducting numerous other classes all over the globe, and the assistant told his boss that it was no longer necessary to tag along as I had demonstrated to their teams that I understood them well. The desired business results were also accomplished faster than expected as the learning was quickly applied within their roles.

There were also some other longer-term benefits. The LO reps said they learned a lot about how to deal better with other executives in the future, and kept renewing my contracts. The client also engaged me as his personal High Performance Coach. We're currently exploring how best to engage some of my fellow Certified High Performance Coaches for group coaching his teams across the globe.

Apply Good Judgment Without Appearing Judgmental

Unlike the examples above, many times I'm brought in to help facilitate a process as a neutral party with no connection to any outcomes. For example, a large client desired a systematic internal process to conduct market intelligence research that could also help external customers. Working with my now-retired associate, Mike Kirkwood, we effectively facilitated a roll-up-your-sleeves workshop with internal stakeholders that produced a succinct process generating broad-based buy-in. Besides Mike having been a founding member of the International Association of Facilitators, the main reason we were brought in was because we had been teaching our own proprietary consultative skills model for years. Now, we certainly could have allowed that to skew our input yet understood how crucial it was to separate our judgment from what would have likely been construed as appearing "judgmental" if we had crossed that line. What are some ways where you might add greater value to a team or project by maintaining that balance between advocating your own judgment vs. appearing to be judgmental to others?

How might that distinction make a difference, you ask? After facilitating many groups experiencing all kinds of dynamics, I was honoured by a US$400 million training services firm as their top Facilitation Partner of the Year, the same year they earned the prestigious Malcolm Baldrige service award. I was later honoured by my peers and the global board to be one of two co-chairs of the 2015 Americas Conference of the International Association of Facilitators. More significantly for you, what situations are you or a team facing where a neutral professional facilitator may assist toward your creating a desired breakthrough? How might it be helpful for YOU to learn and apply consultative "finesse" in any and every work (or family) situation?

Whether you currently manage people or teams, and/or are subtly working your way up within any business culture, I invite you to contact me at info@optimire.com and visit www.consultativeskills.com for a complimentary video series and downloadable "Team Ethics Analysis Model" ebook. I have a ten-year business visa to work in India as well as regularly conduct long distance coaching and consulting engagements in many time zones. Let's explore your needs together.

Rolf M. Foster-Jorgensen

President Optimire Consulting and Training, Inc.
Canmore AB Canada
info@optimire.com   www.ConsultativeSkills.com

Learn from Rolf's 30+ years as a global lead consultant, trainer, facilitator and Certified High Performance Coach to Fortune 500 clients and entrepreneurial teams.

Rolf was awarded as the top "Facilitation Partner of the Year" by a US$400 million Malcolm Baldrige service award winner.
He served as 2015 Co-Chair of the International Association of Facilitators Americas Conference.
Rolf is an inaugural member of global Certified High Performance Coaches, and personally invited on stage twice by the High Performance Academy founder to share coaching tips based on his extensive experience and insights.
Rolf provides interactive e-learning, rigorous case studies and participatory classroom instructional design services, and Train-The-Trainer (T3) events.
He is creator and master facilitator of Consultative Skills, and co-creator of Internal Consultative Skills with marketing and communications emphasis.

He authored Team Ethics Analysis Model ebook, and created the Business Empathy Tool, SituationalALERTness^{SM} and Challenge ExecYOUtive^{SM} products/services for all audiences.

Rolf has also designed, developed, and delivered courses in consultative project planning, project management, market management, complex solutions selling, customer service, facilitation skills, leadership coaching and hardware/software planning.

He and his wife owned multi-million dollar businesses with 150+ employees.

Rolf 's hobbies include playing timpani and Latin percussion in various bands and orchestras as time permits.

Clients include: IBM, Cisco, General Motors, the International United Auto Workers Union, Chrysler, Ford-Volvo, BP/Amoco Oil, Navistar/International Truck & Engine/Monaco Coach, Hewlett-Packard, Yamaha, Abbott Labs, American Airlines/US Airways, Nissan-Infiniti, Motorola, Agilysys, Fluor, Pfizer, small businesses, state/municipal government, not-for-profits, Native Indigenous tribe.

Watch for early release notices about Rolf's upcoming Risk-Giving^{SM} book. It presents a different business operations model that greatly honors employees at every level, while encouraging high performance behaviors by all. People managers and team leaders, of any title, will particularly appreciate how collaboratively rewarding their roles can be in a Risk-Giving^{SM} environment.

STARDOM BOOKS

ABOUT THE AUTHORS

This is a book written by industry experts, each contributing a chapter. Here's a list of all the CO-AUTHORS of this publication (in no particular order):

Lora Polowczuk
Ramakant Sharda
John Terhune
Sreekumar Vadakkeppat
Dr. Emily Letran
Shekhar Vijayan

Faye Kiteriev
Seethalakshmi
Douglas Kong
Shane Ram
Diana Dentinger
Rolf-Foster Jorgensen

STARDOM BOOKS

www.ingramcontent.com/pod-product-compliance
Lightning Source LLC
Chambersburg PA
CBHW031921240526
45464CB00021B/629